FROM GOD'S MONSTER TO THE DEVIL'S ANGEL

Table of Contents:

Acknowledgements	-3
Dedication	-5
Pannie Cakes	1
Chicago Exodus	8
Bloody Texas	12
Introduction to Street Life	29
Death Wish	35
My Gun! My Rules!	44
Waiting On DCFS	51
NFL Awards	55
Home Less	65
Gang Affiliated	75
Lil Yummy	83
Deadly Streets	86
Guardian Angel...Ret.	95
RIP Lil Yummy	107
University Woes	108
Jail Bird	118
Bad News Woo	132
Grounded	137
Murderer!	153

Acknowledgments

I would first like to acknowledge the power of God. God has used me, and I pray will continue to use me to inspire others to escape the street life.

I want to give a big thanks to fellow International Brotherhood of Electrical Worker, Mike Strohecker. You kept pushing me to tell my story, so that I may inspire others. It was your passion that inspired me.

Thank you to author G.P. Ching, for getting me started and sharing your knowledge of being a writer with me.

Shareef Mohammed, mere seconds before I would have been riddled with bullets, you decided it was not my time to die. You literally stepped in the middle of our conflict and somehow got the men to put down their guns. If you would not have intervened, I would not be alive today. I owe you my life. Thank you.

I have to give a big thank you to Kathy Whitlow. Your input with my memoir was invaluable. I value you and your family's friendship, love, and opinion. Love you guys.

I want to thank my sister Ginnie for pushing me in my work. The abuse you suffered eclipses any abuse I have endured. I am amazed by your resilience and ability to still have faith in humanity.

To my sister Kim Pitts; I thank you for all of your constant prayers while I was in those Chicago streets. When I gave up on life, you kept telling me to hold strong and hold on to God.

I want to give thanks to the Director of the Bloomington/Normal JATC, Renee' Riddle. I owe my career to you. Thank you for being there for me in my time of need. I love you.

To my little brother Jeremy Johnson; thank you for looking after my son at Arizona State University. Even though he is miles away, I feel overly secure knowing that he has someone like you to watch over him and reinforce how a man is supposed to conduct himself. We may not share the same parents, but our bond is as strong as any family tie. If you ever need me, all you have to do is call on me. I love you little brother.

To Robert Davis; I am the parent I am today because of you. I thank God every day for putting you into my life. To say thank you is not enough. There is no way I could ever repay you for your wisdom, kindness, honesty, leadership, patience, bravery, and most of all love. I didn't deserve your intervention, but you sheltered me anyway. You took my guns, you took me away from the gang life, you took this homeless kid off the streets, and you taught me how to stand upright as a man. It took a while, but I got it! As a man, I can admit that at times I am still lost without you. In tough times I still turn to your advice for guidance. I always think on how you would handle a situation. I talk about you all the time. You might not have been my biological father, but you loved me like I was your own. I am a representation of you. I carry your teachings. I LOVE YOU DAD! Rest in Peace.

To my wife; thank you for your support, strength, devotion, and love. You are a wonderful wife and mother. I thank God for a wife who keeps me balanced. We work so well and communicate so well with each other. Thank you for being a mother who practices what you preach. The last thing a child needs is a hypocrite for a parent. You are my soul mate. You are the one person that I could not live without. I love you with all my heart and soul.

To my sons; I live for you. I love you. A good father raises his children to be caring, compassionate, faithful, honest, a leader, to be more successful, smarter, happier, and overall to be better person than he was. I pray that one day; you raise your children with the same aim. And if you do, then that will make me the best father in the world. I love you guys.

Dedication

Reliving the abuse, homelessness, and gang life was very painful. Putting these words together so others may read them, brings about feelings of deep shame. I wrote this book with the intentions of inspiring youth in similar situations not to settle.

I am dedicating this book to the youngsters that see gang life as their only option. This book is for the individuals who believe drug dealing is a better choice than attending school and obtaining a degree. Gang life and drug sales are a guaranteed avenue to incarceration and death. The things that matter most in this world are hard earned. Nothing comes easy including; respect, honor, marriage, family, education, a career, financial stability, and a comfortable retirement.

My wish for the youth is that you refrain from obtaining a criminal record and excel in academics. These will be the main factors which you will be judged by. These two factors will guarantee a prosperous future; unlike gangbanging and selling drugs. I also dedicate this book to the individuals who have no experience with gang life, but see it as something to imitate. Individuals in gangs portray their lifestyles as being exciting and glorious. It is simply a coping mechanism to justify their abysmal lives. People in the streets want out, but are oblivious in the ways to escape. The streets are terrible. Only someone not from the streets would see it as something to glorify…take it from me…there is no glory in it!

I also dedicate this book to anyone who is a victim of abuse. I kept silent about my abuse because I feared retaliation. To this I say, even in the face of possible retaliation, you must not be silent. If you allow your fear to silence you, then you are an unwilling contributor to your own abuse. Speak out, and if it doesn't help, then speak out again. Continue to ask people for help until you receive it. For the people who turn their head, you are just as culpable as the abuser.

"PANNIE CAKES!"

    I was hungry, broke, and stunk. It had been days since I had showered. I was living in my car. It was close to midnight. I needed money in the worst way. I was driving around Chicago; looking to rob a crack dealer…any crack dealer. With the money I could buy some food. If there was enough money left over, I could rent a cheap hotel room for the night. I saw my victim selling crack in the alley. He was alone and waiting to sell to his next trick. He was a slender, black man, in his mid to late twenties. I drove four blocks down so I wouldn't attract the dealer's attention.

    I parked my car on a side street. I had to stay in the shadows. I jumped fences and used the darkness of the alley to creep behind him. I shoved the gun in his lower back and told him to, "Empty your fucking pockets!" He responded by whipping around and stabbing me in my left side with a knife. I stumbled back, gasping to catch my breath. Before I could regroup, the man came back at me with the blade. He was about to stab me again.

    I fired, hitting him twice in the chest. This was the first time I had shot someone. It was either me or him. When a person gets shot, it is nothing like in the movies. People don't fall coordinated or gracefully, but rather flop clumsily to the ground. The first thing they do is beg for you not to kill them. The blood doesn't run neatly into the streets. It initially rushes out; until it saturates every part of clothing it touches. The victim's breathing is not regular. Every breath is forced and painful. It seemed as if every breath was hastened and devoid of a natural rhythm. Out of fear of getting spotted I immediately retreated, leaving the man to lie in his own blood. As I ran away I could hear the man faintly screaming, "Help me! Help me!" I didn't get a dime from the man. I was out of breath from knife that was just inserted into my left ribcage. I was in too much pain to run. I pressed the stab wound with my left hand, in an attempt to slow the bleeding, as I painfully jogged to the car. The scene would give the toughest man nightmares, but I wasn't a man, I was another psycho raised on the Chicago streets.

    Days afterward, the stab wound became seriously infected. The wound started oozing puss and began to really stink. The pain was unbearable. It hurt to breathe. I couldn't go to the hospital out of fear of getting linked to the shooting in the alley. I became sick for almost a month. My wound needed stitches, but I knew I couldn't go to a hospital. I kept wrapping it with gauze to keep the laceration closed. I could feel my heartbeat in the wound. Painkillers and ointment that I stole from the store did little to help, but the cut eventually healed into an ugly scar along my left ribs.

    I never intended to shoot the man in the alley. It didn't bother me that I had to. I constantly told myself, "He was breathing when I left him, so he had to be alive." This wasn't the life I chose. I didn't ask to be born. God gave me my terrible parents. God was the one who allowed me to be born in Hell. Since I was born in Hell, God has no right to be upset that I adjusted so well to the fire!

* * *

    Before I go any further, I should probably tell you how I got to this point. My name is Luther Butler. I was born in the winter of 1975 in Chicago, Illinois. My mother's name was Sandra Ruth. My father's name was Floyd Butler. My father was thirty-five when he began an intimate relationship with my drug addict mother, who was sixteen. Aside from being nearly twenty years older than my teenage mom, my father was still married. He and his wife had two children. The oldest child from that marriage, a girl, Telly, was about the same age as my mom. My father divorced his wife and kids for my mom. My mother already had my sister, Jen, by another man, when she was fifteen.

When I was born, my mother was seventeen. My parents had my brother, Dexter, two years later. My father married my mother before Dexter was born. Floyd Butler had seven or eight other children by several different women; most of those siblings were also close to my mother's age. Floyd Butler by every account was a very athletic, muscular, intelligent, charismatic and a handsome man. He would often entertain people with stories of when he played for the Chicago Bears. He had a smile that could light up a room and had a knack for making people like him.

My mother Sandra was a very pretty woman. She was light skinned, with caramel eyes and long hair. I don't have a lot of memories of my early life or my mom. I never understood why my sister, Jen, didn't live with us. My mother was a housewife. She took care of Dexter and me, tended to the household duties, and cooked the meals.

When I was five, I remember Mom making the best shrimp curry. I used to sit in the kitchen and watch her cook. I loved it when she made pancakes. They were my favorite. She was tickled at how I called them "pannie cakes". When I was six, I pulled a chair to the stove and tried to make them myself. They tasted nothing like my mom's. Mine were charred to a crisp. After that, I learned to turn down the fire and have been cooking ever since.

Sometimes Mom and Dad would go in the room and minutes later you would hear her screaming, "Oh Baby! Oh Baby! Oh Baby!" Curious, I cracked the door and saw my dad on top of my mom, while she was yelling the 'Oh Baby Song'. I had never played that game before. I tried playing it with my three-year-old brother. Both of us clad in pajamas, I told Dexter to lie down on his back, then I laid on top of him and we both yelled,

"Oh baby". After about thirty seconds we got bored and never played the "Oh Baby!" game again . . . at least with each other!

I used to go everywhere with my mother. Often, we went to dirty, dangerous places. I remember the men talking to my mom in the same manner my dad would. She received their verbal cat calls and sensual touches willingly. I used to hate it and I hated them. I remember wanting to fight those men to protect my mother. She used to speak to the men in code by spelling the words out so I wouldn't understand. The conversation usually ended by them telling her to drop me off and hurry back.

One time my brother and I were with my mom in an apartment. There were several people there. She told us to go to the back of the apartment so the adults could talk. About thirty minutes later, one of the men answered a knock at the door. He ended up with a gun in his face and my father was at the other end. The next thing I remember was my father telling us to go downstairs and my mom saying she wasn't leaving. He beat her so bad that her shirt came off. It wasn't the gun or the beating or my mom screaming that affected me the most. It was the fact that my mother's breasts were exposed while he was dragging her down the stairs.

Older family members often tell me that when I was young, I stayed by my mother's side. I hated it when my father would hit her like he hit me. My little brother was only three so he didn't get hit…yet. I remember fearing my dad, but loving him.

We had two humungous mastiffs named Torch and Ringo. They both weighed well over 150 pounds. If they peed in the house, they got the same type of beating my mom and I received. On several occasions, I recall my mother pulling my dad off me, pleading with him that I had enough.

One time there were several rectangular shaped items, wrapped in plastic wrap, on our living room floor. Inside appeared to be dry blades of grass. I was only five years old. I didn't know what marijuana was, but I knew it smelled funny. Curious, I poked my finger through the plastic wrap. That was a day my mother couldn't get my dad to stop beating me.

I was six when I started to grow angry. I began imitating the violence I saw from my dad and on TV. I was in kindergarten and my brother Dexter was in preschool. When kindergarten was out, my brother's preschool would allow me to stay in their classroom until my mom picked us up. One day, in Dexter's preschool class, I pulled out a razor blade (our house was full of them) and cut a Latino boy's arm several times. Blood was everywhere. I didn't want to hurt him, but I was so angry. I just lashed out. I wasn't allowed in Dexter's classroom again. That was the first time I understood why I was getting an extension cord to my back.

My mother divorced my father when I was six. She was granted custody, half of his money and half of his antique car dealership. I can't recall what happened to her apartment, but I remember us constantly sleeping in different apartments with strange men. We spent a lot of time at my great grandparents' house, where my sister Jen lived. I loved being around my older sister.

Sometimes we would see our Uncle Mason Jr. or Aunt Patty at my great grandparents' home. Even though they were siblings of my mother, they never really interacted with my brother and me. Every time we left my great grandparents' house, I wanted our sister Jen to go with us. I didn't understand then what was going on, but I knew my sister was unhappy.

I was never comfortable being in that house, especially when my great-grandfather was around just us kids. I remember a time when I went into my sister, Jen's, room and she was masturbating. The fact that I interrupted my eight year old sister didn't deter her. I couldn't comprehend sexuality but I knew something was wrong.

Sometimes we would visit my grandparents on my mother's side. My grandfather was Mason Sr. We called him Popsie. My grandmother was Virginia. I rarely saw my grandfather because of his work hours. We had to be quiet during the day when we were over so he could sleep. If we weren't quiet, we were told that Popsie would wake up and he would 'get us'. Being quiet during the day is an insurmountable task for four and six-year-olds. Even though we were restless, we usually behaved.

There was a time that Dexter and I got a little boisterous and woke our slumbering "Popsie", but he was as nice as could be. Now my grandmother was a whole different story! I made the dreadful mistake of calling her grandma. And she went on a tirade about how she was too dazzling to be a grandma. Calling her grandma was worse than calling a bulimic fat.

Once while we were visiting, there was an attractive, scantily dressed woman on a commercial. Every man in the room stopped talking and stared at the television. My grandmother dashed out of the living room and returned five minutes later in a bikini, high heels and a fur coat. She then proclaimed that she was still sexier than that lady in the commercial. She whipped her head towards me and announced, "Don't ever call me grandma! I am too sexy to be a grandma. From now on you call me Foxy or Foxy Grandma."

"Foxy" seemed more like an older sister than a grandmother. She was witty, loving, and a ball of fun. I felt loved and safe around her. I was too young to notice in all that humor and vitality, that there was a coping mechanism of sorts. I was told of the catalyst for my grandmother's arrested development some years later.

Within a few months we were living with my father. My mother smoked, snorted, and injected herself with too much poison to take care of us. Her drug habit had a hold of her and getting high took precedence over her kids. We were just in the way. I didn't want to leave her and didn't want to be away from Jen and "Foxy". I was terrified of my father. I loved him but I knew the beatings would continue.

I missed my mother like a drug fiend needing another hit. I would ask if my brother and I could visit her. My father would tell me that if we left to see her, we would have to continue to stay on the streets with her. He said that we wouldn't be allowed back. My brother was too young to care either way. That is when the nightmares started. I had the same nightmare three to four times a week into adulthood. In my nightmare, I was trying to make my bed. The bed had thousands of wrinkles. I would try to make the bed neat for my mom by straightening all of the wrinkles. But the wrinkles kept coming back. All the while, my mother's omnipresent voice would be laughing in this creepy

"Huh-Huh-Huh" tone. It might not sound very scary but it woke me up with the sweats. If I went back to sleep right after I awoke, the damn nightmare would start over. Unfortunately, my brother and I were stuck living with my dad and there wasn't a thing I could do about it. It would be eleven years before I saw my mother again and twenty-six years until I saw my sister, Jen. Thirty years later, I saw "Foxy", but unfortunately, Popsie had already passed.

By the time I turned seven, my father left permanent marks on my body from the beatings. Punching, slapping, and extension cords were his weapons of choice. I often wondered why nobody helped me. My brother wasn't getting beat so all my father's anger was directed towards me. I was very independent, tough, and I questioned a lot. All of those traits upset my father and caused me to get beat even more. I started to become bitter and laconic, never speaking a word if my father was around, which angered him more. Dexter quickly learned out of fear to kiss my father's ass, or to tell on me, to avoid the beatings I received.

CHICAGO EXODUS

It was the fall of 1983. I was not quite eight years old and my father was broke. He packed us up and moved my brother and me to his place of birth, Oklahoma. His son and daughter from the previous marriage were elated to have their father back in their lives. They were over our house quite often. It was cool to hook up with my sister, Telly, and brother, Kalen.

In Oklahoma, I discovered that I was athletically inclined. I used to play tackle football with guys much older than me. I was perplexed that my older brother Kalen never wanted to play with us. Kalen avoided sports. One day I was in the house playing Pac-Man on my new Atari. My brother Kalen wanted a turn. He tried hard to beat my high score. When Kalen lost his last man he screamed and put the red-handled joystick in his mouth. He then started sucking up and down on it. I didn't want to play with him anymore. I didn't understand that he was imitating sucking a dick, but I knew he wasn't like me.

While my father was away, my sister Telly took care of my younger brother and me. Telly would bathe me and many times she would get into the tub with me. It was mortifying to see her naked, but I was just a kid. I tried not to notice her glistening breasts bobbing in the water.

Even though Telly was older, she spent a lot of time with me. She always had a guy around. There was an instance when I was with her and her boyfriend. I can't remember what I said or did, but it must have pissed her boyfriend off. He told Telly to bring me to him and she did. He hauled off and hit me in the face, knocking me to the ground. I saw stars, but didn't cry. I stayed on the ground attempting to catch my breath. He told her to stand me back up. When she did, he slapped me down again. This happened two to three more times until finally I cried. They both warned that if I told, I would be the one who got into trouble. I was scared to tell anyone, so I held it inside.

That moment fueled my already ignited inner rage. It was the start of my justification to hate people. I didn't hate her boyfriend. He had no allegiance to me. I hated my sister Telly. She was the individual who I expected to keep me from harm. I expected her to care for me. How could she allow her friend to hurt me? My hate was the only thing that I have never been able to let go. And frankly, I didn't care to.

I never forgave Telly for that day. Unfortunately I was forced to be around her because we had the same father. Telly had a boyfriend named Bradley. We were frequently at Bradley's parents' house. His dad was Nolan Richardson, head basketball coach of the Tulsa Golden Hurricanes. He later became the head coach of the Arkansas Razorbacks and coached them to a National Title.

Nolan had a pretty wife who looked Hispanic. We called her Aunt Rose. She made the best French toast ever. She called it 'Superman French Toast'. She made French toast for my brother and me for breakfast, lunch and dinner. We didn't care what else she could cook because we couldn't get enough of that damn French toast! Uncle Nolan seemed nice. He was quiet but I felt safe around him. Many times I wished Aunt Rose was my mom. They lived in a nice big home. I think that is why we were over there so much.

Since my father was born in Oklahoma, the majority of my family was there. During this time, Dexter was still the youngest of my father's children. I was next youngest. It was in Oklahoma that I really found out what kind of man my father was. He used his status as a professional football player to have sex with any woman who was fascinated by his stardom. My father had kids by at least five different women. He never stuck around to raise any of them. We got to meet our brothers Jon,

Floyd (he was named after our father but rumors are that he is not our dad's child), and Kalen.

The oldest brother, George, lived in California and refused to have any contact with our father. The abuse his mother suffered by the hand of our father caused George to have some serious apathy towards our father. I had a lot of sisters in Oklahoma as well; Kim, Deborah, Telly, and Cheryl. Some of my siblings had kids as old as or older than I was. How in the hell am I seven and I have a seven-year-old old nephew calling me uncle? It still feels weird to this day. It was the first time that I remember meeting many of them. Some of them said they had seen me once when I was younger but I couldn't remember. I recall meeting my sister Cheryl. She looked just like my father. She was dark skinned with full lips and long hair. I remember her being so pretty. She was exciting and fun. She paraded me around all her friends and I loved it. I loved all my brothers and sisters (except for Telly), but I was partial to Cheryl, because I spent more quality time with her. She was my escape.

Cheryl lived with her grandmother. We called her Big Ma. She was a fusser, a screamer, and a yeller. She talked just like Owen's mom on the movie 'Throw Mamma from the Train'. Even through all the yelling and fussing, I loved to be around her. The only bad thing about Big Mamma was that she kept a blood thirsty Chihuahua on her lap. That dog wanted you to touch or hug her so he could literally bite a chunk out of your ass. That dog wasn't just mean, that dog was the damn Anti-Christ!

I got to meet my uncle Jewing. I believe he was a preacher. He was tall and solid like an NFL player. He was so nice, and he seemed to genuinely care for my dad. We met our aunt Dolly as well. It was a brief meeting but remembering her sweet potato pies still makes my mouth water. Those pies had to be great because I was seven the last time I tasted one.

My father always told us in private that Uncle Jewing was a child molester. Dad always had something bad to say about all his brothers and sisters. I used to believe that he was trying to keep us from bonding with them, so he told us horrible stories about them. He talked bad about his siblings behind their backs, but to their face he was Mr. Friendly and smilingly accepted any help they offered.

We stayed in Oklahoma less than a year. Right before we moved, my father had to go out of town for a week. My father was leaving Monday morning right after the bus picked my brother and me up for school. He was to return Sunday afternoon. Before my father left, he told me that his brother would be picking us up at home after school.

The bus picked us up in front of our house in the morning to take us to school. After school, the bus dropped us off back at home. We went inside the house, had a snack, and waited for our uncle. I didn't have contact numbers for any family members so I couldn't call anyone. Dexter complained that he was hungry, so I sliced some hotdogs and fried them in a pan. I washed the dishes and we watched TV. Around ten PM, I put my brother to bed and got us ready for school the next day.

This routine continued for about three days. We got tired of fried hot dogs, so I did what I knew best, pancakes for supper. While watching television, I happened to see a lady making peanut butter cookies. They looked good, so I wrote down the ingredients and the steps. I mixed all of the ingredients and I baked the cookies. My brother and I loved them.

A few more days went past and my father returned home. Much to my father's surprise, my brother and I were home as well. He asked where our uncle was. But, we didn't even know which uncle was coming to get us. He asked me what we ate. I told all the things that I cooked. From then on, my father had me cook the majority of the meals and clean-up. My brother would help with the dishes when he turned older.

My father did nothing in the house from that point out. I swept, washed dishes, cleaned the toilet, cleaned the bathtub, mopped the floors, and I cooked. He had a bed tray so that he didn't even have to get out of bed. After I cooked, I would put the food on the bed tray, while he watched television. I tried to cook the best meals to appease my father. When my father was frustrated, the abuse was unbearable. Cooking and cleaning seemed to alleviate the bloody admonishments . . . a little.

BLOODY TEXAS

After a several months of living in Oklahoma, we moved to Texas. My father told everyone in our family we were leaving because he bought a chemical manufacturing plant in Houston. We picked up and drove to a really nice area of homes. We pulled up to beautiful house and a black couple came out. A man picked me up and hugged me. My father said, "This is you Uncle Curtis." He was married but I cannot remember his wife's name. I do remember her being extra sweet and loving to us. They had a pretty little white poodle name 'Muffin'. I loved living with them. The abuse immediately disappeared.

One day Muffin was hit by a car. Uncle Curtis' wife was a complete wreck. Muffin was bloody and yelping at the top of her lungs. They rushed Muffin to the emergency veterinarian. Days later when the vet released Muffin, two of her legs were in a cast and she had stitches running the full length of her ribs. She was basically immobile.

Uncle Curtis and his wife had day jobs. They left Muffin on a dog mat where she could eat and relieve herself. Without even thinking I would pick Muffin up and take her in the backyard to go potty. I did this about every hour or so. I remember the first time my uncle and his wife returned home.

FROM GOD'S MONSTER TO THE DEVIL'S ANGEL

They asked why Muffin hadn't gone potty on the disposable mat. I told them that I had taken her outside to potty. Uncle Curtis' wife showered me with kisses. That was the highlight of my life. I continued to do that until Muffin was out of her cast. That dog followed me everywhere after that.

I noticed when there were people that truly cared for us; my father refrained from being abusive in front of them. I just got regular whippings with a belt. He was careful not to draw blood or leave marks. Later my father moved us out of my uncle's home and into an apartment. I never saw my uncle and aunt again.

Now we were in Houston, Texas all alone. The physical abuse began immediately. I don't know what my father did for money but he definitely didn't own a chemical manufacturing company. We lived in a lower class neighborhood complex.

Floyd Butler made a lot of friends in Texas. One thing about my father, he was handsome, muscle bound, and he could sell water to a whale. Everyone loved him. To keep my father appeased, I put extra effort in the meals I prepared. I made shrimp fried rice, stir fried vegetables, and other things many adults cooked. I made my father a two layer strawberry cake. He bragged and told everyone what I did. Women that he knew came over and couldn't believe a seven-year-old could do that. When that excitement wore down, the beatings continued.

I remember that we didn't have money for clothes. We did a lot of shopping at Goodwill type of stores. One escape from our state of destitution was playing basketball. The basketball court was about a mile from our apartment. I would play basketball all day during the summer. My brother Dexter was still a little young, so he would watch or play around the court with the other smaller kids. One day I found a pair of jogging pants that were left on the court. The jogging pants were in mint condition. I brought them home to show my dad. I wore those pants to play basketball almost every day.

Once, I took the jogging pants off, like I usually did to play ball. After we were finished playing, the pants were missing. I went home to tell my father that the owner of the pants probably took them back. Before I could get the whole story out, he punched me in the chest. I fell backwards into my father's closet. When I stood back up my father yelled, "You just gonna step on my fucking shoes?" I rushed to exonerate myself by telling him I didn't mean to step on his shoes; rather his punch catapulted me onto them. That was a big mistake. He said, "Oh you want to talk back?" My father punched me in my face and I was knocked unconscious for a few seconds.

When I came to, I staggered to get to my feet and out of the closet. While I was unconscious, my father left the room. He returned with his extension cord and instructed me to exit the closet. The closet would have hampered his ability to fully swing the plastic coated, cat-o-nine tails. I came as told. My father hit me at least fifteen times with the extension cord. My skin split after the second lash. It seemed as if every hit made him angrier. The more I cried, the worse the beating became. After the beating was over I sat on my bed for about an hour, until I knew he wasn't coming back. I pulled the blood soaked sheets off of my bed and placed them into the dirty clothes hamper. As I was doing so my father yelled, "Soak those in the tub!" His instantaneous and loud adjuration startled me, and caused me to jump.

My blood stained bed sheets were the least of my worries. I sat too long in the clothes that I was beat in…big mistake. The blood started to coagulate so my underwear and my shirt were stuck to me. After carefully and painfully peeling them off, I went to the bathroom to check my wounds. A few of the lacerations were close to needing stitches. I couldn't believe how badly I was injured and became enraged. I no longer loved my father.

I walked back into to my room, feeling broken inside and out. I heard my father conversing on the phone. He was laughing with a lady like nothing happened. I was so upset that I yelled, "I don't know why I got a whipping in the first place!" I heard him tell the lady, "Hold on, I will call you back." My father stomped to my room replying, "Oh! You don't know why got whooped!" I steadfastly replied, "No sir!" My father in turn returned with the extension cord and hit me about ten more times. I winced and sucked in air through my clamped teeth, but I did not cry. He asked, "Do you know now?" I replied, "No Sir!" so he continued to lash me with the extension cord. It seemed to go on forever.

I finally started to cry. While I was being punished like a slave, one lash from the extension cord struck me in my temple. I remember seeing stars and hearing a buzzing noise in my head. That lash numbed my whole body. I had never felt like that before. I thought I was about to die. Fearing my imminent death, I immediately stopped crying. I was trying to get a grip on what was happening to my body. My father stopped whipping me. He was amazed that I had stopped crying and was staring right at him. He thought I was crazy, but I was just trying to figure out if I was dying, about to faint, or what. The beating was over. He walked away with a stunned expression mixed with slight fear.

That summer I started to play little league football. I was eight years old. The team I played for was called the South Main Mustangs. I was short and fast so the coaches tried me out at cornerback. The coaches told me to hit anyone who tries to catch the ball. I was a natural for that position. I was so short that they never saw me coming. But I was so compact that the collisions were like train wrecks. I injured an offensive player every game.

Texans love their football. Different men would give me five or ten dollars after every game. It was nothing for me to leave a game with fifty to seventy dollars. For an eight-year-old, I was rich. My father would take the money and tell me he was putting it in the bank for safe keeping. Occasionally college coaches would let me know that my name was in their mental databanks and they would be keeping an eye on me. We ended up going undefeated and winning the championship for the freshmen division.

Football was my escape and I was great at it. My father bragged to everyone about my athletic ability. He did it in a way which lead people to believe that he bequeathed to me all that he knew of football. He acted as if he showed me how to play, when he really didn't. He told everyone about his brief stint with the Chicago Bears and how I was good just like him. I hated when he bragged on me. I was not proud of him. I was not happy to be his son. When people found similarities between us, it would sicken me. I was nothing like him. It was bad enough that I look like him.

I played for the Mustangs the following year. During practice, I noticed that I was wheezing and couldn't breathe very well. After practice, I went home to tell my father that I couldn't breathe. He told me that I was out of shape and it would get better. Unfortunately I couldn't fully breathe for the next few days. I went to my father again but this time he was upset. My father said, "Stop whining like a little faggot!" He asked me, "Are you a punk? Huh? Are you a fucking faggot?" I answered him with the same polite response, "No sir". He retorted, "Then why are you whining like one?"

    I kept telling my father I couldn't breathe. My father said, "I know what you need." He returned home with an enema bag. He told me to take off my clothes and go into the bathroom. When I entered the bathroom naked, I noticed a red bag filled with water. It had a long white tube and a pointed white plastic tip on the end. He told me to lie on my side on the cold tile. I did as he instructed. He put Vaseline on the white plastic tip. My mind was racing. I know he's not going to put that in my ass! I kept thinking, "I know I am only eight, but what does my butt have to do with my breathing?"

    He slipped the tip into my rectum. My father flicked a clasp and water went rushing into my anus. The water was a little too hot. It was hurting my stomach. I wanted to tell him it hurt but I was scared of the backlash. It kept going and after a while my body couldn't hold any more water. I told him that it hurt and to please stop the water from flowing. He became upset and told me to stop acting like a pussy. He emptied that whole bag into my stomach. I was moaning and squirming in pain. He told me to shut up and hold it! He kept eyeing me, so I did what he said. He stood over me for another ten minutes and finally told me to sit on the toilet. When I jumped towards the toilet, fluid started gushing from my ass to the floor. I knew I was going to get hurt for that, but he just told me to clean it up. From that point on, it seemed like I was getting enemas every month. I started to keep my ailments from him because he looked for any reason to shove that plastic tip in my ass.

    My wheezing continued. By the end of my second season with the Mustangs my coach brought me home to tell my father that I probably had asthma. He told my father that he should take me to a doctor. My father acted all concerned. As soon as my coach left he chastised me for running to my coach about my breathing. To shut me up he went to the store and came back with an over the counter asthma medicine called Primatene Mist. When I took that medicine, it actually made my asthma worse. It also made my lungs hurt. I told my father and he took the Primatene Mist from me and told me that I must not have asthma. My lungs hurt for days. I just kept the wheezing to myself from then on out.

Now it was official, I lost faith in people. I was competitive athletically. I detested bullies and had no problem fighting them. Two of the toughest guys in our apartment complex were brothers. Their names were Kevin and Jermaine. Kevin was a year older than me. Jermaine was three or four years older. One summer day Kevin was trying to fight everyone. We were playing dodge ball. If you tagged Kevin out, he would try to fight you. He was muscle bound and aggressive. My competitiveness wouldn't allow me to give him a pass. I tagged him out. He squared off on me and cursed me out. He tried to punch me but people got in between us.

As tough as I was, I only had one previous fight. My father made me beat up a boy threatening me when I was six. I wasn't sure if I could beat Kevin. I saw Kevin beat up a few guys so I had a respectful fear him. As soon as Kevin had another chance, he rushed me. He swung widely but missed. Kevin then assaulted me with several blows to my head and body. The fact that I was still standing after his barrage of punches gave me confidence. I picked him up and slammed him. I hit him on the ground a few times. Kevin's older brother, Jermaine, kicked me off his little brother. I ran home, put on my football helmet and football pads, and returned. Jermaine probably could have still easily beaten me, but he was a coward. He ran home crying and returned with his dad's bullwhip and a knife. Luckily adults intervened by this time.

I didn't like the grammar school I initially attended. It was a lot of corn-fed bullies there. I had to be careful not to stir these big boys up.

In school, I was the vagrant looking city boy that no one liked. I was quiet in school. I really had no friends. I didn't participate in any sports. I was a respectful kid oblivious to the toll my depression was taking on me. Nobody liked me because I never let anybody close to me. I was so quiet that my peers found me creepy. My clothes were subpar hand-me-downs and my personality reeked of insecurity.

While in middle school my achievements were average at best. Houston's school districts were easy. There was nothing challenging about them. I rarely studied but I could maintain passing grades.

I couldn't focus on studying, because I spent most of my time at home avoiding my father. One day I was beat so bloody that I couldn't take it. My teacher was a nice lady that I felt that I could trust. During class I went to her and asked her to come in the hallway. She followed behind and I showed her my bloody wounds. She started crying and hugged me. She then took me to the principal. The principal was a middle-aged black man. She showed him my bloody underwear and wounds. The principal sent me back to class. Within the next few days the principal called my father to have a meeting. I wasn't in the meeting. I don't know what my father told the principal, but no action was taken. At the end of the school day I was petrified to go home. I arrived at home with my father waiting on me. He said, "You telling your teachers on me now?" I told my father that I didn't tell on him. Out of fear, I lied, saying that the teacher saw some of the wounds and asked me how I received them. I thought he was going to beat me to death. But he never touched me.

On a separate occasion, my class had a big project to make a collage of Africa. Our assignment was to have our parents get some magazines and cut out pictures that represented Africa. Then we were to take those pictures and paste them onto a cutout poster board that was shaped like the continent of Africa. I told my father of the assignment. He told me that he was not buying new magazines simply to cut pictures out of it. That was my father's way of saving face. We didn't have money to buy a magazine to deface. I had to come up with an alternate way to complete my project. There was no way I was speaking to my father about the project again.

When the day came to turn in our projects, I had none. The bus ride to school was dreadful. As soon as they tell my father that I received a zero for a missing assignment, he is going to kill me. I was the last one to exit the bus. To my surprise, there was a collage lying on a seat. I checked the back of the collage and saw that there was no name on it. I picked it up and wrote my name on it. I turned the project in and received a grade of 100. Unfortunately for me, the paper was so good that the teacher posted it up on the wall for all to see. It was right in front of the class, on the A-Plus Board.

About a week later the kid who actually completed the assignment went to the teacher and indicated that the assignment was his. The principal summoned both of our parents to the office. My dad was in the principal's office again, but this time it wasn't to discuss my abusive wounds. I lied and said the assignment belonged to me so an investigation ensued. The boy's parents had every magazine they had used to complete the assignment. I remember my dad telling the principal, "See? I told you he was bad?" The principal slightly nodded in the affirmative and we left. What you do in the dark will come to the light, and I knew my dad was about to light my ass up when I got home! Of course the extension cord tore into my skin. It was a terrible beating. But I always took a little solace when I knew I actually did something to get punished.

I never missed an assignment again. I still never asked my father for help. The very thought of doing so resonated a pain within the pit of my stomach. We had one more research assignment. We had research using books and encyclopedias. I did all the research myself. The assignment was to be a page long. My report was three pages. I was very proud of myself. This paper was a large percent of our grade. The morning the assignment was due, I awoke feeling confident. I had an extreme sense of pride. Most kids needed their parents to complete the assignment. I completed it all by myself. I gulped down my cereal. I waited for my little brother, grabbed my assignment and got on the bus.

When I arrived in class, I reached in my folder to turn in my assignment. Wait! This cannot be! Where is my assignment? I told the teacher that I really completed it. The teacher allowed me to retrace my steps back to the bus. I never found the report. The walk back to class was like walking to my own execution. I returned to tell my teacher that I could not find it. She carried a look of skepticism and rightfully so. Not too long ago I had stolen an assignment and claimed it as my own. With tears I pleaded with her. She said I could turn it in the next day for a lesser grade.

I went home and tore up the house for my assignment. My dad saw me searching and asked what I was doing. I told him that I was searching for my missing assignment. He never saw me doing any research so he automatically assumed I was lying. He snatched me up and beat the hell out of me. During the beating I kept proclaiming that I completed the assignment, which made him whip me longer and harder. My chastisement left me bloody again. I was broken. I had actually tried hard. But I was weighed, measured, and found wanting.

I couldn't take it. I remember immediately going outside, looking up to the sky and cursing, "Fuck you God! Fuck you. You think I will pray to you? Fuck you! You gave me these parents! You allow me to get beat! Since you won't help me, I will do the Devil's work!" I stopped praying on that day. I also started having repeat nightmares of my father beating me to death. So not only do I have nightmares about my mother mocking me, I have to deal with the night terrors of dying by the hands of my father.

In the middle of the school year, my dad ended up moving us to a nice apartment complex. This new place had an upstairs and a downstairs. My brother, Dexter, and I still shared a room, but the place was way bigger. Dexter was now getting an extension cord to his backside. He was seven. Dexter was very timid and deathly afraid of our father. We used to get extension cord lashings for everything. If we broke a glass, we got whipped. If we used the wrong knife to make peanut butter and jelly sandwiches, we got beat.

My brother couldn't take the whippings, so often when my father found an infraction, my brother would beg me for help. He would cry in a whisper begging, "Oh please oh please help me!" The majority of the time I would tell our dad that I committed the infraction, and I would take the abuse for my brother. I wanted my father to hurt me instead of my little brother. I loved Dexter and protected him at all costs. Plus, I knew my brother was weak. The more my father beat me, the more my resolve was to one day be away from him. I used my father's blood thirsty corrections to fuel my anger for him. It made me stronger and more independent of my tyrannical father.

I befriended a short, pudgy friend who lived two blocks from me. His whole family called him Nino. He lived with his mother. Since he was an only child his mother spoiled him with toys and food. I loved being at his house. I played Super Mario Brothers over his house during my free time. Nintendo and Cabbage Patch Dolls were the toys to have back then. My father never bought us any toys. He never bought us any Christmas presents or birthday presents. He said that Christmas was the white man's holiday propelled by commercialism. What the hell does that mean to a young kid? We enviously watched kids every Christmas open their new toys and clothes.

I started two businesses that summer. One was collecting aluminum cans and turning them in to the recycling shop. The other was washing cars. I tried lemonade, but that is more of a thriving business for cute white girls. Nobody wants lemonade from a short, ugly, scarred up black kid. Customers kept asking me if I washed my hands. I had two people under me; my younger brother, Dexter, and Nino. I had them place little rocks in the cans before we crushed them, so they would weigh more. We got paid by weight and we did really well. We couldn't keep up with the carwash business. Cars kept coming all day. I paid Nino's fat ass less. He always needed to run home and get a snack! At age nine, I had at least $50 in my pocket at all times.

I asked my father for my mother's phone number and address. I called her, but the phone number was disconnected. I bought some earrings from the corner store and mailed them to the address my father gave me. Within a few weeks my mother called to tell me she loved the earrings. She told me that she loved me and missed me. She would tell me stories of how she always had me with her.

I hadn't seen my mother in years but I loved her just as much. Hearing my mother's voice was like a high. I sent her earrings every week. She would talk to Dexter, but he didn't show the same enthusiasm as I did. Dexter was probably too young to really remember her. Then my mother would talk briefly to my father. He always tried to get her to come to Texas for sex. Yeah I was nine, so I knew what the 'Oh Baby' game was. By the end of the summer I saved up enough cash to purchase my mother a plane ticket to Houston. I gave my father the money to purchase the ticket. I really wanted her to visit us. She said she missed me, so why not fly her down here? I was short on the plane ticket so my father agreed to pay the rest.

Before my father purchased the ticket, he called my mother to tell her. I was so excited that I hid right by his door to listen to the conversation. I could even hear her responses through the phone. He told her that he was going to purchase her a ticket to fly to Houston. My father told her that she would stay with us. I heard her say she was scared he would beat her again. She told him that she wanted to just see her babies. My father then said, "If you're not gonna be with me, then you not gonna be with them!" I heard her crying and then my father hung up.

I hastily snuck to my room and cried. A few minutes later my father called my brother and me into his room. My father told us that our mother was still a drug addict and she couldn't be trusted. He said she is going to get the ticket and buy some crack. He said that he knows she is not coming and that she didn't love us. He didn't know I heard the conversation. I was so angry at him. I cried right there. Upon seeing me cry, my father said, "I know, that's your mother." I wanted to say, "Bastard, it is you!" I was hurt. I stopped sending my mother earrings. I didn't talk to my mom for years after that.

The nightmares about my mother continued on a regular basis. I didn't even recognize that for a while, I wasn't even having them. Now they were back and terrifying as ever. I still had the nightmares about my father killing me as well. Sometimes in the nightmares he would beat me almost to death, other times he would stab or shoot me. I always woke before I died in my sleep. I would wake up drenched with sweat and with a pounding headache.

School started, and now we attended a new school. The school was called T.H. Rogers. By this time I was really quiet, but boy was I a hustler. I had $30 in candy in my book bag. I sold candy to everyone. By the end of the week, my $30 turned into $90! Every one called me the 'candy guy'. I didn't have friends but in my mind being a customer was better than being a friend. In class, a bully in my grade made a point to fight me. He stared at me. He teased me about my clothes. He had groups of people laughing at me. But I wanted no parts of him. He was built like a young bodybuilder. This guy kept yelling how his family was from 5th Ward. I didn't know what it meant but by the students' reaction, I had an idea.

One day I was holding the door for the kids behind me. After everyone went through the door, I let the door go. About ten seconds later this same bully ran up behind me and said I purposely tried to close the door on his little sister's finger. I apologized, even though I saw no sister in sight. But, in mid apology, he punched me in the mouth. My top lip swelled instantly. To say I was enraged was an understatement. My dad might abuse me, but nobody else! I put him in a headlock and punched him more times than I could count. I was crying the whole time. His whole face was swollen and partly bloody. When the teachers intervened, it was the kid from Chicago who was disciplined. I was detained in the office until my father picked me up. I won the first fight. I knew that I would not come out the victor in the second altercation with my father and his extension cord. It didn't matter that I was protecting myself. All that mattered was that I was in trouble. I received an extension cord along my backside until my father got tired.

It was November and I noticed that we were not eating right. Our food supply in the house was low. I never saw my dad working. I wondered what he did for money. Thanksgiving Day came and there was a knock at the door. My father opened the door like he was expecting someone. Was it my mom? I was anxious. But to my surprise it was a white family. They never came in the house but they were handing him things. It was so much stuff that he called us to help. It was a cooked turkey, dressing, pies, and all the fixing of a Thanksgiving meal.

What the hell was going on? Are we broke? What about this chemical manufacturing company my father supposedly purchased? Didn't he play for the Chicago Bears? Where was all that money? He did own an antique car restoration business, but all he talked about was how my mom got that in the divorce. I was very embarrassed. Did anyone see us getting handed this food? On Christmas Day, the same exact thing happened. But this time it was multiple families. Some handed us food. Others handed us bags of presents. Oh my God! We got Christmas presents! There was no embarrassment in that. Our first Christmas was from another family… a family that didn't even know us. We tore through those presents. My father who didn't believe in Christmas tried on a watch and a nice sweater, too. He was such a hypocrite.

The school year ended without any more conflicts. It was the beginning of summer. I was starting up my car washing and can crushing business again. As we were collecting cans, a group of kids approached us. It was several kids. They kept yelling they were from the 5th Ward. I didn't know these guys. Hell…I have never even been to 5th Ward! They all looked rough. Then, from the back of their group approached the guy I fought earlier in school. This was the liar that said I tried to slam his sister's finger in the door. He said, "Remember Me? I have been working out." He then made a muscle. I put up my fists and they all exclaimed, "Dayuum! That nigga got heart!" He backed away from me in a manner that showed he didn't want to fight.

All the guys with him were older. So they kept teasing him and calling him a little sissy. They left without any altercation. I was scared out of my mind. When I turned around, I noticed that Nino was gone. I didn't even hear his fat ass run off! I definitely wouldn't have attempted to fight if I would have known he had left. Dexter was no help at all. I probably would have tripped over him trying to fight.

I walked to Nino's house to see what happened to him. He told me that it was too many of them and that he wasn't going to get beat up. A few weeks had past and the fifth ward crew caught us outside again. This time it was more kids my age, and a humungous girl. She looked like a boy and was built like Ray Lewis. She snatched the boy I previously fought in my face. She told me he was her cousin. Then she turned to him and said, "Fight him or I am gonna fight you!" As he approached me in a pugnacious manner, she yelled to him, "Don't worry, if he gets you this time, we all jumping in!" I am screwed! Nino's fat ass was already running! My brother and I ran. We tried to make it to Nino's house, which was about three blocks away. As we reached Nino's house, I heard a "click". Nino was just on the other side latching his wooden privacy fence. I exclaimed,

"Nino! Unlock the gate! Let us in!" He said "no" and ran into his house.

A few seconds later, the 5th Ward crew caught up to us. The boy who I had months prior, delivered him a generous ass whooping walked up to me. His crew formed a semi-circle around us. My brother Dexter and I were backed against Nino's privacy fence. None of them paid any attention to my brother. He couldn't even pretend that he was about to help me. I felt overpowered, outnumbered, and stuck with a handicap...my little brother! My opponent's female cousin, who resembled Ray Lewis, grabbed me by the throat. I started to cry. I told them that I didn't want to fight all of them. One of the older guys in the crowd told them to leave. They all patted the boy on the back like he was a conquering hero and left.

After it was over, Dexter exclaimed, "I can't believe a girl made you cry! I thought you were supposed to be tough!" He said it as if I was a coward or something. As we were walking home Dexter mockingly asked, "Why did you cry when they wanted to fight?" I replied, "Because you were my backup!" He was so scary; with the proper coercion he probably would have helped them kick my ass! For years, when my brother wanted to say something to insult me, he brought that incident up. I never gave him or anyone else another instance to do so.

Since we left Chicago it seemed like my father had a different woman every month. It was the same thing but with different women... they would have sex and leave in the morning. But they never hung around much longer than a month. There were so many ladies that I never attempted to connect with them, even though I wanted a mother figure in my life more than anything. I sometimes reminisced about a lady he dated in Oklahoma called Carlita. She stayed with us for several months. She always stroked my face and called me honey. She was beautiful. She used to be a model. She was about six feet tall. She had a short haircut, elegantly styled with semi-full lips. Her voice was a little deeper but in a sexy, womanly way. My dad had her crying it seemed like every weekend. She would always beg him not to break up with her. She loved him and loved us. I can still hear her crying, "Bullet please...I love you!" One day I guess Carlita gave up and left. In Houston, I thought about

Carlita a lot. Carlita and everybody else referred to my father as "Bullet". I think people called him that because of his football speed.

I had lost all faith in God, even though we attended church every Sunday. We actually attended a very prosperous church. The pastor was very versed in the Bible. He was able to teach it in a way that actually hit home and made sense. There were very rich people who attended our church. Warren Moon of the Houston Oilers attended. My father was friends with Warren and his wife. I can't remember if they had any children. I remember Warren keeping a mean look on his face.

One day after church my father picked us up from Sunday school. On the walk to the car I overheard my father telling a group of adults about an incident that just happened in church. He went on to tell them that Warren Moon had slapped his wife in the face so he intervened. Did I just hear my father correctly? This is the same man who got off on making women cry over him. This was the same monster that I saw on several occasions beat my mother like they were reenacting a scene from the 1993 movie 'What's Love Got to do With It'! That made me so mad at him. What a hypocrite!

While in church I literally ran right into Hakeem Olajuwon of the Houston Rockets. He was so tall that my short ass didn't even reach his hip. When I ran into him I apologized. I reared back my head and exclaimed, "You are Akeem Olajuwon!" He replied, "Yes...I think so" and smiled at me. Back then he was Akeem Olajuwon. During the NBA off season, we used to go with my dad to the gym and watch him play basketball with Akeem. Almost all the guys there were NBA players. I remember Olden Polynice was there. He was drafted by the Chicago Bulls but was traded to the Seattle Supersonics. I think I remember seeing Kevin Johnson and Charles Barkley a few times as well. Even though my father was a football player, he was a pretty good basketball player as well. I guess pro athletes all hang together.

I started to see a lady at our house a lot. Her name was Fran. She was about the age of my real mother. She was one of the most beautiful women I have ever seen in my life. She was about five feet tall. She was dark skinned and had full, long hair.

Fran was built like a model. She dressed very nice. Fran could have had any man she wanted. I didn't know what she saw in my geezer of a father. He had to be at least twenty years her senior. She was quiet and really liked my father. She started to spend the night a lot. I actually enjoyed cooking and bringing food to her. She didn't eat my food, but her polite refusal didn't bother me. For some reason, my father didn't stop abusing us when she was around. He was happier so the abuse lessened. If Fran came over right after we were beat, she would tell us that our dad was a good man and that he loved us. I replied to her one day saying, "I don't love him." Fran replied, "No! You're only nine. Don't talk like that!" But even at nine, I knew that I didn't love my father. He beat all my love for him out of me.

    I ended up becoming a child who was unknowingly battling depression. I wasn't a trouble maker. I was always respectful. But I was a ticking time bomb. I would get so sad that I wouldn't eat for days. I literally wanted to die. I felt as if someone gave me a drug that caused me to feel sad and sluggish for days. I also took any signs of disrespect as a reason to hurt someone. I was extra polite to people to avoid conflicts. I felt anybody who messed with me deserved to be hurt…or even killed! One day, I would muster up to strength to kill my father.

    I was playing a pickup game of football with the neighborhood boys. After the game a guy started to tease me. I barely knew this guy. We got nose to nose as if we were about to fight. He punched me in the face and ran. I chased after him but he was too fast. He made it to his house and locked the door. He continued to tease me through the glass pane of his wooden door. I got so mad that I punched through the glass and hit him in the face. I noticed he was cut really bad in his face. Blood was gushing from his forehead. I was scared because I knew I was in for a beating. Then I looked down and noticed blood by my right shoe. I happened to look at my arm and it was cut worse than his face. I could see my vein! Our parents rushed us to the hospital, but not before we fabricated our story. We said a guy threw a rock and it broke the glass pane on the door. We claimed that the glass shards lacerated his face and my arm. I think they knew better but my father never said anything else about it.

Home is supposed to be one's safe haven. Growing up, home was the last place I wanted to be. I remember my brother and I returned home from playing outside. When we entered the house my father was displaying a scowl. As soon as we entered the apartment he yelled, "Hey! Which one of you forgot to wipe off your placemat after you ate?" My brother and I dreadfully walked over to see who the culprit was. It was where Dexter had eaten. We both made sandwiches before we went outside.

My lazy brother neglected to wipe his food mat off. Dexter always did stuff like that. I apologetically took the blame, but that wasn't enough. Our father went on a tirade about how disrespectful the act was. After his tirade my father asked me what I had to say for myself. I told him that it was a mistake, and I attempted to wipe up the crumbs. He then said, "Oh! Just a mistake! Who in the fuck do you think you are talking to?"

My dad went upstairs for the extension cord and returned. He told me to turn around and put my hands on the table. Before I knew it, I felt the first lash on my neck and head. I cried and exclaimed, "Dad, you hit me in my face!" Then I turned around to show him the bruise mark on my cheek and forehead. He yelled, "Turn your ass around!" and punched me in my face! The vicious blow knocked me halfway under the table. I stayed there in hopes that the table would shield me from the lashes, but my father pulled me by my leg from underneath. That beating seemed to go on forever.

After the abusive episode, my father went to pick Fran up. As soon as he left, I grabbed my backpack, put some clothes in it, and ran away. I walked for hours in the direction that I believed my Uncle Curtis lived. I was hoping to recognize the scenery and eventually make it to the safe haven of my uncle's. About two hours later, my father and Fran pulled alongside of me. I cried as I crawled into the backseat of the car.

INTRODUCTION TO STREET LIFE

By the end of the summer, we were moving back to Chicago. My father accepted a teaching job in the Chicago Public School system. I was so excited to be moving closer to where Popsie, Foxy, Jen, and my mother lived. While on the road, I broke my silence with my father. I hit him with a barrage of questions. I asked where my mother was. I asked about Jen. I inquired if we could see Foxy and Popsie. My father was obviously irritated at the factors that inspired me to break my monk like vow of silence. My dad vengefully answered every question I asked.

My father started by reiterating to my brother and me that our mom was a drug addict. He said she had been on drugs way before him. He went on to say that my mom probably uses drugs to dull the pain of her grandfather's repeated molestation of her. My father alluded that Jen's parents could possibly be my mother and my mother's grandfather. He went on to say how messed up my mother's side of the family was. He continued to tell me that not only did my mother's grandfather molest her but he also molested his daughter, my grandmother, "Foxy. Then he wryly chuckled at the fact that my mother allowed her daughter, Jen, to live with the same man who molested her and her mother.

My father vengefully told me that my great grandmother knew her husband was molesting his family members. I couldn't believe what I was hearing. Was any part of this story true? My mind was all over the place. Is my sister ok? Why did my mother leave Jen with that sick man? Did my great grandmother know about this? I was so upset with my father for making light out of the situation, even if he was telling me the whole truth. Why would my dad take us to my great granddad's house if he was such a bad man? My dad spoke with him. My father laughed at his jokes. This was sick.

My father ended the conversation by telling us that our mother didn't love us…she only loved her crack cocaine. I wanted to say something positive about my mom but before I could, Dexter blurted out, "I don't want to see her anyway!" What an ass kisser! He was too young to remember the good things about my mom. Dexter wasn't even going to give our mother a chance just to appease his despotic father. I shot my brother an evil look and went back to my laconic ways.

We moved to the south suburbs of Chicago. We initially moved in the house of a man named BJ, his wife and their son. All of them were tall and big boned. My father told us that BJ was a teammate of his from the Chicago Bears. BJ was extremely nice. His wife was very pleasant as well. Their son was spoiled, huge and a bully. He didn't like the adolescent intruders in his home. Their son had at least three years, a foot, and ninety pounds on me. He yelled at me and pushed me around a lot. BJ never disciplined him.

One day all the neighborhood kids had a huge tackle football game. It was so big that the parents came to watch. BJ's son was known to be one of the best players so he was picked first. I was so tiny that I was picked last to play. I was on the same team with BJ's son. We had played for thirty minutes, and they never passed me the ball. We were getting our butts kicked. Out of desperation, and nobody else to pass the ball to, the quarterback passed me the ball. I juked and ran until a scored a touchdown. The kids and adults went crazy. They were in awe every time I touched the ball or made a tackle. BJ's son was obviously jealous, and rightfully so. There was a new Sherriff in town!

BJ talked about how good I was until we got home. His son was pissed. His son really treated me like shit from that point on out. One day the kids were home alone. I got hungry and decided to cook. The eye on the stove wasn't lighting. BJ's son didn't cook, so he was shocked to see me light a match to light the stove. I blew the match out and threw it in the trash. He then ran over, turned off the stove and pushed me. He said we were not allowed to cook or use fire. When all the parents returned, he told them what happened. I told them what I was doing and that I cooked a lot. I received praise for cooking at such an early age from BJ's wife. That praise sent their son over the edge. He yelled, "He could have burned the house down!" and pushed me. I pushed him back and he started punching me. I was so pissed that I never felt any of his punches. I returned punches and landed several in his face. BJ finally broke it up. I obviously got the better of the exchange. BJ pulled his son back who was so mad he was shaking. BJ let his son go. He acted like he was going to attack me again, but probably knew he would receive more of the same. His son just stormed to his room. This is when I really took noticed that not only did I have courage, but I was tough as well. We only stayed at BJ's house for a few weeks.

One day while I was taking a shower, my heart started beating so erratic that I lost my breath. Out of extreme fear, I nakedly ran to my father, informing him that I was having a heart attack. My father responded by saying it was normal. I was so scared that I demanded he take me to the hospital. He called me a sissy and never took me. After the first occurrence, I continuously experienced erratic heartbeats several times a week. My father never took me to a specialist to get it investigated. After a while I became desensitized and accustomed to the dysrhythmias, even if it knocked the wind out of me. It wouldn't be until I became an adult with insurance of my own that I saw a heart specialist. Because of years of ignoring the problem I had incurred irreparable heart damage. The condition caused by my faulty heart valve was attributed to my mother's drug use, when she was pregnant with me.

My father, Dexter and I left BJ's house for the south side of Chicago. We stayed on 71st and Coles. My father took a teaching job at Bryn Mawr Elementary on 74th and Chappel. It was a rough school. The neighborhood wasn't the best either. My brother and I were bussed to John Hope Elementary on 55th. That school was in a gang warzone. A lot of those gang wars were fought in and around the school.

I was ten years old and scared of my father. I was positive that I was going to die of a heart attack by the time I was eleven. I was in serious need of a friend. This new school could be the very place to bond with someone more like me. School had already started so I was the newcomer. I immediately became the class clown to win over friends. Much to my dismay, my attempt at becoming the funny kid backfired. I made the girls dislike me and it made the tough guys want to fight me. I was always in trouble for talking, which meant a beating when I got home.

The subculture in urban Chicago had its own set of norms. The majority of those who resided on the south side are in the middle to lower socioeconomic class. Many people who fall into this socioeconomic rung would display material possessions in attempt to mask the fact that they were broke. In urban African American Society, many people are more concerned with what you drive or what you are wearing versus a person's future goals or an individual's integrity. This plight further compounded my predicament. Not only was I the new kid, but my clothes were from resale stores.

Because I was short and stocky, my clothes never fit me. Comments were always made about my clothes. My dad bought our shoes from Payless. Jordans were the big thing back then. People were literally murdered for their Jordans. I didn't want Jordans. I just wanted any shoes that could stop me from getting teased. They could have been Converse, Diadoras, Adidas, British Knights or Filas. I was just tired of the negative attention my clothes brought. I remember my 5th grade teacher, Mrs. Johnson, left the room for a minute. This guy in my class named Jerry told the class he was going to turn off the lights to see if my shoes glowed in the dark. He turned the lights off and the whole class laughed and made fun of me. I got teased like that almost every day.

Across the street from John Hope was a house. That house was occupied by the street gang called Vice Lords. About five blocks from there were Gangster Disciples. There were also

Black Stones in the Mix as well. They fought, shot, and pulled out guns on each other in front of the school all the time. Sometimes to avoid being killed they would run in the school. Imagine at ten years old seeing someone get shot or chased with a gun almost every day. I was so screwed up that I adjusted easily to the violence.

Before school the kids used to play together. Some played ball. Some played king of the hill. I played games with the kids every once in a while, but I mostly stayed to myself. Almost every day this man would come in the morning with a boom box blasting Rob Base's single, "It Takes Two". He was a Gangster Disciple. He openly carried a gun in his back. All he did was continuously walk in a circle around the school in the morning with his boom box. He was basically letting the Vice Lords across the street know that if they came outside, he would kill them. As he walked around the school almost all of the kids followed him like he was the pied piper. Sometimes you could see the guy put down his boom box, pull out his gun, and go after a known Vice Lord that he spotted. Of course they would run. The Gangster Disciples were the largest organization in Chicago. Sometimes the Vice Lords would gather up and go after the GD's. They were a smaller group but they were just as deadly.

One morning the boom box gangster was walking around John Hope. All the kids were following him as usual. While this was going on two men in their late teens or early twenties walked up to me. They introduced themselves as Tony and Hosea. They were Gangster Disciples. They asked me why I sat alone and why I didn't follow that guy around like the rest of the kids. I simply told them that I wasn't impressed. They told me how dumb they thought their fellow GD was behaving. They taught me to never bring attention to myself.

I am still not sure exactly what they saw in me or what about me interested them. Every morning they showed up at the school and taught me a little more about street life. They both told me how they jointly owned a cleaners and how they laundered their dope money through the cleaners. They taught me about saving my money. They even told me about shooting someone. They said in a shootout most guys get frantic and miss everything they shoot at. They said that is how innocent people get shot. They told me always stay calm.

The last pieces of advice they told me was simple, "Boys fight and men kill! If it is worth fighting over, it is worth killing over." They instructed me to kill anybody I fought; no matter if I won the fight or not. Tony told me, "Never leave someone a chance to come back and kill you…kill them first!" I absorbed all of their teachings. One day I noticed that I hadn't seen Tony or Hosea in a few days. They left as abruptly as they entered my life. But those months of tutelage prepared me for the streets. I knew I didn't want to be a Gangster Disciple. They had too many people that joined them because they were the largest organization. In Chicago, they are not called gangs, they are called organizations.

My father always told my brother and me stories about men pulling guns on him. He showed us a bullet wound on his stomach. He said a guy shot him but he still took the man's gun and beat his ass. I knew my father lied a lot, but I believed this story. He had the bullet wound to prove it. My father spent many days with his friends speaking of gunfights and coming out the victor in battles with opponents who were seemingly unbeatable. I ingested every story he told. I trusted these behavioral tactics and treated them like the Gospel. I believed that was how a man was supposed to behave. There was shooting around where I lived every day. It was nothing to see someone shot or killed. Kids our age that we hung out with were sometimes killed in the crossfire. All these things coupled with my father's stories hardened me.

DEATH WISH

My father had his new teaching job, but we were still very broke. One of my friends was an obese teen named Mikey. He used to watch drug dealers' cars for money. Mikey took pity upon me because I didn't have any toys, so he brought me in. I also began watching the drug dealer's cars for money. After a while, I had enough money to buy a Chicago Bulls hat. It was a black hat with the words 'Chicago Bulls' in rhinestones. When I was eleven I was walking with Dexter (9), Kevin (11), Michael (12), and Michael's little brother Dee (9).

We were all coming back from Rainbow Beach, which was about eight blocks away from our apartment. We were only a few blocks from our apartment when we came across twenty boys about my age and older. They were staring at us from across the street. From the group, what appeared to be a ten year old boy approached us. He asked us why we beat up his brother. I told the boy it wasn't us and to have his brother come over so he could verify it. A boy who appeared to be a little older than me ran across the street towards us. His right hand was holding an object that was tucked into the front of his pants. I assumed he would look at us, recognize that we were not the perpetrators, and walk off.

When the boy, whose hand was tucked in his trousers, reached me he pulled out a revolver and put the gun to my temple. At that exact moment the little boy that asked if we beat up his brother snatched the hat off my head. It was a damn setup! I was pissed. As soon as that bastard snatched my hat, I picked him off his feet and slammed him into the gated fence behind me. The guy with the gun said, "Don't make me kill you!" I slammed his little accomplice again. He took the gun from my head, cocked it, and put it into my ribs. I still didn't let go. I was waiting for Kevin and Michael to jump the guy with the gun. Kevin had no intentions of helping me with this robbery. Michael called my name and said, "It's not worth it dog. Give them the hat." I hesitantly released my grip. The gunman for some reason quickly backed away from me. I think he knew I was gonna try to take the gun. I would have unloaded every bullet in the chamber if I would have taken that gun from him.

I stormed home and one of the older men from my block noticed the frown on my face. He asked, "What's wrong lil man?" I told him what happened and he ran in his apartment. He came running down seconds with a hand canon! He said let's go get your hat back. We walked down 75th looking for the punks who had just robbed me. One thing to understand about 75th was that it was a war zone. It was nicknamed "Terror Town" because it was known for its murders. I still to this day can't believe I walked that block looking for revenge! Twenty people armed with assault rifles couldn't stand a chance of making it out alive, let alone one boy and an armed man! But I was loyal. I would have died with him that day.

Thankfully, we didn't run into anybody, let alone the cowards that took my hat. The older man walked me back home and I thanked him. When I went into my apartment my father was waiting on me. My sycophant brother told my father what had previously transpired. As soon as I entered the apartment my father yelled, "Are you fucking crazy? Do you have a death wish? Now you are fighting guys that pull guns on you?" I was really confused. I thought that was how a real man was supposed to behave. I also learned that Dexter was a snitch. He wasn't telling because he was worried. He was telling in his typical kiss his father's ass fashion.

After I was robbed at gunpoint, my personality started to change. I became self-destructive. I started to become more like the thugs on the street. A corner store sold starter pistols. I bought one. The thing looked like a real gun. I carried it around everywhere. It gave me a sense of empowerment. Having that gun further enhanced my psycho personality. The kids used to watch me put a couple of blanks in the revolver, spin the revolver, put it to my temple, and play Russian roulette. Their facial expressions were that of amazement and fear. It gave me a euphoric sense of pride to see their expressions when I pulled the trigger.

There was a city transit train called Metra that passed through 71st and Exchange. I used to amaze the kids how I would run over the tracks just in time not to be hit by the train. I recall one attempt where I didn't quite clear the train. The train clipped my right heel and spun me four feet into the air. I landed violently onto the ground. I was bruised, yet full of adrenaline. I celebrated my near death experience by yelling at the top of my lungs. The kids couldn't believe it. I didn't know it at the time but I had a true death wish. I thought I was just being exciting. My brother, still in his effort to bond with his dad, told on me that I was running in front of moving trains. My father didn't reprimand me. He just said I had a death wish and walked away shaking his head.

My father worked the summer school program at Bryn Mawr Elementary. He took us with him because they served lunches. We had fun there. I bonded with a lot of kids. After about a month I got kicked out of the program for hanging all the way out of a second story window. That embarrassed my father so bad that he beat me until he got tired. I deserved that, and I accepted that beating.

While living on 71st and Coles, my dad had a visitor. It was a familiar face. It was Carlita! It was nice to see her. She was so happy to see us. She came over and immediately started taking care of us. Carlita worked for a pharmacy in Chicago. When I would return from playing outside, Carlita noticed that I was wheezing and short of breath. She believed I had asthma so she brought home a prescription inhaler. It knocked out my wheezing by the 2nd puff. She fussed at my dad for letting me have an exacerbation for that long. I loved the fact that a motherly figure was sticking up for me. Carlita stuck around off and on for about a year. As usual, my dad kept making her cry. I would see her crying a lot because she did want to break up with my father. When she left, Carlita still sent me asthma medicine. It really hurt me when she finally departed from our lives. I deeply cherished our bond.

After Carlita, my father dated this lady named Diane. She was very religious. She was about average looking in the face, but I remember her hour glass shape. She must have told my father that we had to go to church with her for them to sleep together. I guess if you have premarital sex with someone in your same church then God will only look at it as a half sin! She was nice. She was really into my dad. She was so quiet that we really didn't get to know her.

I remember an incident during one of Diane's visits. My father must have been having a really bad day. Dexter used a serrated knife instead of a butter knife to make a peanut butter and jelly sandwich. I remember him getting hit with the extension cord and trying to run. That pissed my father off so bad he beat my brother for about two minutes straight. The only reason my dad stopped was because Diane buzzed our apartment. He put the extension cord up and sat with Diane in the living room.

My brother coward and cried in my room and it broke my heart. I thought to myself, "This is not right!" I told my brother, "I am going to tell him that he shouldn't have whipped you!" Dexter agreed. I said, "Come on" and I pulled my brother by the arm. I lead my brother to the living room where my father and Diane were conversing on the couch. Dexter, out of fear, snatched away and stopped in the hallway. I kept going. Upon entering the living room, I told my father that my little brother didn't deserve the beating he had just received. Diane kept her head down as if she didn't hear a word.

My father out of embarrassment tried to ignore me. Then I said, "A man should never beat a kid for such a small thing!" My father hopped up and told me to go in the kitchen. Dexter ran and hid. My brother wanted no parts of what was to come. Upon entering the kitchen my father grabbed two knives. He handed me one of the knives. My father said, "Since you think you're a man, we are going to fight like men…to the death!" With the knife in my hand, I looked him in the eyes. He knew I was truly contemplating my next move. My father said, "Come on! I want to kill you so bad that my dick is hard!" But I chickened out. I was too young and still questioning my ability to defend myself against my father. I couldn't do it. If I thought I could have beaten him, I would have stabbed him to death. I dropped the knife and started crying. My father hurried and walked back to Diane like nothing had happened. The apartment was small. I know she heard because she left shortly after that. She usually stayed for hours or even the night. He got rid of her soon thereafter, just like all the rest.

After Diane departed, our father informed Dexter and me that a lady he dated in Houston would be moving in with us. He said she had a son and a daughter close to our age. We later found out the lady was Fran. I was happy to know it was her. She was nice to us in Houston. We never knew she had kids, but that was a big plus. I might have someone to talk to. I never conversed with my father. I literally said two phrases to him, "Yes Sir" and "No Sir".

Fran had a son, Terrance who was the same age as Dexter. She also had a daughter, Tiffany who was about two years younger than Dexter and Terrance. Initially the living situation was rough. I began to grow jealous of Fran's kids. I started being rude to Fran. I began to grow frustrated with the separate rules for us and her kids. They had nice clothes and nice shoes. We didn't. Fran worked for a clothing store so every once in a while she would bring my brother and me nice things. But she made sure her kids were sharp. We got beat, and Fran's children didn't. Fran wouldn't let them be struck by my dad or an extension cord. If they acted up, they would get a hand or sometimes a belt on the backside. Fran's children were barely ever whooped. Dexter and I were beat on a regular.

At the time, my father really didn't like Tiffany and hated Terrance. Terrance had no problem displaying either verbally or through body language that he didn't care for my father's antics. Terrance didn't speak to my father and tried to avoid him as much as possible. My father thought Fran's children were spoiled. I think what really upset him was his inability to control them. I loved Tiffany with all my heart. I was partial to her because of my sisters. She hung with me. She even slept on my chest a lot. She knew I would protect her at any cost.

Tiffany, Terrance, and I hung out together. We all had the same feelings for my brother Dexter. We didn't trust him. I believed his survival mechanism allowed him betray us at any cost. This kept him in good graces with our father. Good graces with my father meant that you didn't get beat. My dad used to play Dexter on that fact. Before Fran's mother passed away, she made it known that she didn't care for my father as well. She verbally announced it on several occasions. Fran, Tiffany, and Terrance lived with us for several months before my father kicked them out. It was in the winter. I felt so bad for Fran, Tiffany and Terrance.

Shortly after my father kicked out Fran, a lady named Bella moved in. She had a daughter. They were from California. Bella was beautiful inside and out. Bella had a daughter who was about five years younger than me. Her daughter was full of life. She wasn't jaded by mistreatment or abuse.

Tiffany and Terrance still came around. They were over almost every day. They moved into an apartment a few blocks away. We missed each other and continued to hang together. We wanted our parents to get back together. We really didn't let Bella's daughter into our circle. Dexter, Tiffany, and Terrance were actually mean to Bella's daughter. I might as well have been mean because I did nothing to help her.

My father used to beat Bella. I witnessed him abusing her a few times and I felt so sorry for her. He used to hit her often. Sometimes my father would make Bella stand in his room with her nose in the corner. My father wouldn't even close the door to conceal the domestic abuse from the children. She got smart and eventually moved out. Bella was such a beautiful woman that when she left my father's friends were in disbelief. They kept asking my father, "How did you let her fine ass get away?" My father informed his friends that he told her to leave because he couldn't deal with her herpes anymore. He was so vindictive. He told everyone about her personal problem. I was so happy for her that she left. She deserved a way better companion...herpes or not.

Fran, Tiffany and Terrance moved back in with us. It was kind of short lived. My father ended up kicking her out about three more times before it was all over with. He always kicked her out in the winter, or when she was low on money. I believe he tried to make Fran suffer as much as possible. I loved when they lived with us because I finally had someone to talk to. The beatings continued but not as frequent. Fran also was an excellent cook. I started calling her mom. Dexter continued to call her Fran. He didn't like anyone who was close to his dad. He wanted Floyd "Bullet" Butler all to himself.

The one thing about living on 71st was all the kids. We played football, basketball, raced, and hung out all the time. There was a group of us that hung together: Kevin, TJ, Jermaine, Michael, Dontario, Wysingo, Brandon, Tiffany, Terrance, Dexter, and myself. Kevin was spoiled and selfish. If you asked him for a piece of his candy bar he would literally get mad and throw it on the ground. His mother was Lori. She was pretty and nice. TJ and Jermaine were brothers. They had very positive and involved parents. Even when their parents divorced, they worked together well for the sake of the kids. Michael and Dontario were brothers. Michael was a good basketball player. His younger brother Dontario was known for crying every time he fell. Wysingo and Brandon were brothers. They had all the toys and clothes. Their parents had money. Wysingo was my age. He was the pretty boy, but he was as tough as they came. I read a karate magazine that had him ranked #1 in the nation for his age group. He didn't look like it, but he could kick your teeth in! His younger brother Brandon was Dexter's age. Brandon was my size and tougher than nails too.

One night Michael, TJ, Jermaine, Dexter, and I spent the night at Kevin's House. His mom bought us pizzas and soda. We stayed up laughing and teasing until four in the morning. Kevin was upset at a joke I told. It was around 4am when he called my father telling him that he wanted me to leave. My father told him to send me and my brother home. All the other kids knew of my predicament by then. They were upset with Kevin and decided to leave as well. They all volunteered to talk with my dad and tell him that Kevin was acting like a spoiled brat. When we got to my apartment they stood at my door trying to tell my father what happened. He said he didn't care and closed the door in their faces. The only thing that mattered was that we disturbed his slumber. He was so upset that he beat Dexter as well.

    At John Hope elementary school, we played what we called war games. The Vice Lords and Black Stones were on one side and the Gangster Disciples were on the other side. The Gangster Disciple side had two leaders. One was a huge guy. He was light skinned and humungous. He had to have flunked a few times. He wore a patch over his eye where he was shot in the face. The second guy's name was Lawrence. He reminded me of myself. His clothes were unkempt. His hair wasn't combed. But he was loyal. He could answer any math question that the rest of the class couldn't. Lawrence was in my class. I felt sorry for him. He could have been anything. But he was damned to be in the streets.

    This is how the war games worked; at any time we saw the opposition, we fought. It was play, but anybody watching would be unable to tell that we weren't fighting for real. I wasn't a GD but I teamed with them. We fought in the halls, during breaks, during lunch, and we even asked the teacher for passes to catch our rivals in the hallway. I gained my respect (from the gangbangers at least, the girls still thought I was a bum) because I could fight. Then the war between the GD's and the Vice Lords got way worse in the street. Now the war games were over. They were killing each other for real.

    Fran was back in the house with us. Terrance still stayed away from my father and Tiffany was still attached to my hip. Dexter was still snitching every little thing to my father, and I still barely said a word in the house. On the last day of sixth grade, for reasons unknown, I took a carton of eggs to school. I had every intention to egg my history teacher's car. I just didn't like her. After exiting the bus in the morning, I saw my history teacher. I yelled to her, "I'm about to egg your car!" ten minutes later I hit her car with an egg. Immediately after I hit her car with the second egg, the school security pulled me into the office.

    The principal threatened to hold me back in the sixth grade even though my grades were above average. I was waiting on the "Grimm Reaper" to pick me up from the office. What was I thinking? I was starting to get so compulsive. But it didn't matter…I would be dead very shortly. I went home to accept the beating of a lifetime. But I knew that I had brought it on myself. I took it like a man.

MY GUN! MY RULES!

    I was twelve years old. The constant abuse had become unbearable. I didn't know which one was deadlier, the streets or my home, but I was about to find out. There was this older teen I liked. She never would have dated me. I was too young, too short, too broke, and too ugly. She stayed a few houses from me. She was light skinned with full lips. She had cat eyes and long hair. Her overly ample breast on her petite, hour glass frame drew even more attention to her. As I was standing outside my apartment, she called me over. She asked if I could escort her to her friend's house on 75th.

    I knew not to walk her. 75th was Black Stone Nation. Where I lived on 71st, was Gangster Disciple territory. If they saw me, they would shoot me just by association. I told her no, which by her facial expression, you could tell that she was not used to hearing. As she begged, "Please?" she put her arms around me, pushed her ample breasts against me, and kissed me on the lips. Twelve minutes and a full erection later, we reached her friend's house. As she entered the gate of her friend's house, she turned to me and said thanks. Wait! No kiss? No breast-filled hug again? What a tease!

    My disappointment would be short lived. The fact that I was on 75th filled my body with a morbid sense of fear. I walked casually as if I belonged there. I kept my eyes on the ground. I walked past a guy who was about my age. He was staring me in my face. I tried to not to make eye contact. He said to me, "What's up Folks?" (Gangster Disciples were known as folks.) I kept walking and didn't reply. He then said, "I know you are a GD, I see you on 71st all the time." It seemed as if everybody on that block turned their attention to me. About nine guys ran towards me and surrounded me. Two guys put their arms around me and forced me to walk with the group. They led me to an alley and interrogated me. They kept asking me if I was a GD. I kept telling them I wasn't. But, I would be damned if one of those guys pointed out my airbrushed Bart Simpson shirt. The shirt depicted Bart Simpson on a skateboard. But the caption by Bart's mouth read, "That's all Folks...."

I knew I was dead. Of all days to wear that damn shirt! One of the guys used his illegal cell phone to make a call. About five minutes later two more guys came. One obviously was their leader and the other was a GD who lived in the neighborhood. He evidently got a pass because he grew up with them. They asked their neighborhood GD if he knew me. He told them no. Their leader took his gun out of the small of his back and wrapped it up in his Jordan Jacket. He put the jacket on the ground and told everyone to play basketball. There was a milk crate with the bottom cut out, fastened to a light pole in the alley. They all got up to play.

Their leader yelled at me in a threatening manner, "You're playing too, Folks!" As soon as the game started my dumb ass competitive nature kicked in. I was scoring, blocking shots, and stealing the ball. I kept stealing the ball from the guy I was defending. They started teasing him by saying, "You gonna let Folks do you like that?" After stealing the ball again, the guy I was defending threatened, "Do it again and I'm going to shoot you in the face!"

What the hell was I doing? I somehow forgot why I was really there. These guys were going to kill me one way or another! I played soft defense and my man began to score. One of the guys on my team told me, "If he scores again, I am going to shoot you!" The GD that came with them didn't play in the game. He sat and watched. When he had a chance he whispered to me, "They are going to kill you! You better get out of here!" Their head guy saw the interaction and snapped at the neighborhood GD, "What you say? Watch your mouth before we fuck you up too!"

I had to get out. I knew I was dead. One of the guys shot the ball and it bounced hard to the back of the alley. While they were following the ball's trajectory, I made my move. I ducked and ran out of the alley towards my house. I was about a mile from my home, but I just needed to get out of their territory. I had to run about five blocks. I had a good ten steps on them before they realized that I was getting my Carl Lewis on! I heard them yelling, "Kill that nigga!" I heard footsteps but I didn't know how close they were. They yelled for assistance from a few guys in the street who weren't with them. Those guys tried to trip and grab me but I juked around all of them. My body started to get numb. I was waiting for the bullets to start crashing through my body. After a while I didn't hear any one running behind me. I never looked back to see if I outran them. I ran almost the whole way home.

    I was real cool with the guys on my block. They all called me the tough shorty. They were all GD's and they were at war with the Black Stones. I ran to where they hung out and told them that I needed some backup. I told them that the Black Stones tried to shoot me because they thought I was a GD. They all kept saying that they didn't believe me. I was known for being honest so I was shocked. They wouldn't even listen to the whole story. Then I figured it out. That was their way to saving face. They were the killers on my block. But they couldn't say that they were afraid to go on 75th because it made them look weak.

The GD's had no reason to help a kid (who was not a GD) that knowingly wondered into hostile territory. One of the GDs asked me, "Do you really want to go kill some of them?" I told him yes and he came back out with a snub nosed 38 revolver. I called his bluff and snatched the gun out of his hand. Every chamber had a bullet in it. The GD pointed back toward 75th and said, "Go ahead." I took the gun and walked in the direction of 75th. As soon as I got out of their eye sight (And they were watching!) I turned the corner and went back to my house.

    I stayed in my room for hours playing with that gun. If my father would have walked in at that time I would have shot him without any hesitation. I was tired of the abuse. I was tired of the enemas. I was tired of being held under the thumb of this sadistic tyrant. I flicked the release and popped the barrel out. I spun the cylinder around then with one hand slammed it back into the gun. Every waking minute before and after school I played with that gun.

The first time that I was totally alone; I pulled the gun from inside of one of my shoes. I went into my brother's room and opened his window. I removed the screen. I aimed the gun at the sidewalk. I pulled the hammer back then I put my finger on the trigger. As soon as I touched the trigger the gun fired. I wasn't ready to shoot yet! The sound was deafening. I wanted to try it again but I didn't know where to get any more bullets. I wasn't going to ask the boy who handed me the gun out of fear that he would ask for the gun back.

There were times when my depression paralyzed me. I didn't want to get out of my bed for days. My body moved sluggishly. I was in a deepened state of sadness. I was sad all of the time. I didn't want to eat. I didn't want to play sports. All I did was lie in the bed. These feelings would come over me out of nowhere. I didn't know what was wrong with me, but I wanted to break this feeling. I had to do something exciting. I took the gun to show my friends. Most of them had never been that close to a real gun before.

I always got a rush showing them how crazy I was. I opened the barrel and took all but one bullets out. I spun the barrel, cocked the hammer, and pulled the trigger. Kevin kept yelling for me to stop. I did that a few times. I then added one more bullet in the chamber next to the bullet I already had in there. I spun the barrel around and pulled the trigger twice. The look on Kevin's face was way different than when we played Russian roulette with the starter pistol. The look on his face actually put fear into me. Kevin's expression actually brought me back to earth. I spent the next few days happy to be alive. I never played Russian roulette again.

It was still the middle of summer when my sister Telly visited with her two children. My father had warned us to be careful because Telly's daughter was molested by Telly's boyfriend. He told us that she was really distrusting of men. My father said that my sister and her man were drug addicts sleeping in their car. They were broke from their drug addiction. He loved when people needed him. My sister kissed his ass like Dexter did. He talked about Telly so bad. My father told everyone in the house, "Watch! Telly isn't even going to have money to get back home. I don't know what's wrong with her ass. Damn shame!" I didn't want to see Telly but I did want to see my niece and nephew. When they arrived I didn't speak to Telly. My nephew Trenton was full of life. He bounced around all day. My niece, Monique, was distant. She was emotionally disfigured from the sexual abuse she endured. She had a stare about her that made me feel uncomfortable. There were a few times that Monique would fake being sleep and watch me through her almost shut eyes. I felt so bad for Monique but I stayed my distance. I was afraid that she might accuse me of touching her.

    My father started a verbal argument with me while Telly was there. He was within ear shot when I told Dexter, "If he touches me, I am going to kick his ass!" Telly, overhearing our conversation, ran into our father's room and yelled, "No you not gonna touch my daddy!" She was trying to coordinate a fight against me. Surprisingly, my father didn't budge. I wanted to hurt them both. He knew that his reign of domination was nearing its end.

    Telly begged her father for gas money to get back to Oklahoma. My father gave her the money and talked about her as soon as she headed home. She would have given her kids away for our father's love and he didn't even respect her.

Shortly after Telly left I was passing by my father's room and overheard him and Fran talking. I heard Fran telling my father that a person looked exactly like him. Then I heard him tell her, "She is not my kid!" I didn't know what was going on but I was about to investigate. Fran and my father left the apartment. I immediately ransacked my father's room to see what all the fuss was about. In his drawer was a picture of a lady. The lady looked exactly like him. She looked like me. I turned the picture over and it read "Deborah Butler" Deborah also wrote him a letter speaking in detail of the short time he was in her life. In the letter Deborah made reference to other siblings. How many kids did my father have?

    A few days later I overheard my father on the phone. I couldn't make it out but it was bad. My father hung up the phone and made another call. I heard him tell someone that my sister Cheryl had been murdered. I could barely fight back the tears. I heard my father tell two different versions of why Cheryl was murdered. I couldn't believe how insensitive my father was to his own daughter's death. He acted all sad to the person who delivered the message. He then turned right around and dogged my sister Cheryl to the next caller.

My father's callousness to my sister's murder further fueled my hatred of him. He told some people that Cheryl and her friend robbed a drug dealer and that the dealer killed them. He told other people exactly what he was told… Cheryl's good friend broke up with her boyfriend. Later, Cheryl's friend began to date another man. When the ex-boyfriend discovered that she started dating another man, he became enraged. He went to my sister's house hoping Cheryl would divulge where this new boyfriend lived. My sister didn't tell him so he cut her throat. After she died he raped her. Somehow the psycho still found out who this new boyfriend was and where he lived. He went to the new boyfriend's house and to his surprise his ex-girlfriend was there. He shot and killed the new boyfriend. He then raped his ex-girlfriend then killed her. After that, the guy went to the park and committed suicide.

A little later my dad received another call. The caller was telling my father that his son, Kalen (the joystick sucker), was dying of AIDS. They told my father that he only had a few days to live, but he wanted to see his father before he died. My father waited a few days, I believe, in hopes that Kalen would pass. If Kalen died he wouldn't have to go to Oklahoma. My father detested homosexuals. Every five seconds he was accusing my brother Dexter of being homosexual. I remember Floyd telling Fran that Kalen only had a few days to live, but he was holding on to life until he got a chance to see his dad. My dad was elated at the notion that his presence willed another person to live. My father hadn't talked to Kalen in years. My father finally flew to Oklahoma. Upon his return, my father always ended his story by telling people, "He wanted to see me more than anyone before he died!" He was so self-absorbed.

I was elated that Fran, Tiffany, and Terrance moved back in. But because of the abuse, I had grown increasingly isolated. I still never spoke around my father. I tried not to eat or drink if my father was around. My father started verbally and physically abusing Fran. I overheard him having a conversation with his friends about a time Fran was kicked out of his house: My father was arriving in Chicago at the airport. Fran was supposed to pick my father up. My father went on to explain that Fran was late picking him up so he punished Fran by slapping her in the face and making her stand with her nose in the corner.

I couldn't believe what I had just heard. She was so nice to me. She was like my mom. One day after my father berated Fran, I told her that if he touches her, that I would kill him. She smiled and gave me a hug as if to say, "Thank You". A few days later my father told me of a conversation that he and Fran had. He said, "Fran told me that if I mess with her that you are going to help her."

I didn't deny it but I didn't reply. I just looked my father in his eyes. I wanted him to try and beat me. I wouldn't even have tried to fight back or escape. I would keep my sobs to myself, which always made my beating worse. After it was over, I would have got my gun and killed him. But my father only replied, "If you ever dream about tangling with me, you better wake up and apologize!" It was the way in which he said it that showed a little fear, or at least a bit of respect for me. I was getting older, taller, more muscle bound, and tougher. The one thing that bothered me was Fran. I told her I would protect her because I loved her. I wanted her to be safe. She turned right around and divulged our secret to my father. I then knew that I couldn't trust her anymore. I knew that she would betray me for my father, even if I had her best interest at heart. That realization gave me unbearable torment.

WAITING ON DCFS

It was the beginning of the summer. I was thirteen years old. I needed a physical to enroll into high school. The nurse performed her usual screen of my spine, blood pressure, and knees. She then told me to remove my shirt for an evaluation of my heart and lungs. After her checkup the nurse called my father over. She pointed to the raised scars on my arms and back. Without looking at me, the nurse asked my father for an explanation about the horseshoe shaped scars all over my body. My father sloppily explained that they happened while I was climbing a fence. He went on to tell her that boys are rough and that those types of scars are normal.

The nurse turned to me and asked me if I received those scars while playing on the fence. This was it. This is my time. I'm about to tell her! As I looked up, my father was giving me the most intimidating glare. I dropped my eyes to the ground and the only thing that came out of my mouth was, "Yes, I did it on the fence." The Caucasian nurse, who was barely five feet tall, grabbed me by my arm. She then told me, "Doctors, nurses, policemen, firefighters, and teachers are mandated reporters. That means that we are bound by law to tell if a child is being abused. There are people who can help." She walked over to my father and pointed a finger in his face. She told him, "If I ever see any more marks on him, I will have him removed from your home and you will be placed in jail!" My father cowardly muttered, "I...I understand what you are saying, but he did do that on a fence!" That little lady gave me courage that I never thought I had. My father was put into his place by a lady who weighed no more than 110 pounds. I knew what my father was doing was wrong. I knew he was a coward and I knew who to go to for help.

I was still having the same dreadful nightmare about my mother. I didn't recognize it until years later, but my nightmares about my father were evolving. They started off with him killing me. I would awake right after he administered the fatal blow. When I turned fourteen, our battles turned into me getting wounded. I would awake after being stabbed or shot. Later my nightmares evolved into me having stalemate battles with my father. My night terrors later evolved to me killing my father. As my dreams changed about my father, so did my fears… or vice versa. I wasn't as scared of him as I used to be.

Fran was in one of her many "kicked out hiatuses" so I had no one to turn to. I can't remember the circumstances that surrounded my beating. But I do remember feeling fed up. The nurse's explanation of mandated reporters resonated within my head. Wait! I know a teacher! Kevin's mother, Lori, was a teacher. I remember because my father helped her obtain a teaching position.

The day after my beating I called Kevin and told him that I needed help. I told him what happened to me. He told me to move in with him and that his mother would protect me. I told my little brother Dexter that I was moving to Kevin's house so I wouldn't get beat anymore. When I arrived at Kevin's house, I asked him where his mom was. He said she was out but she would be back in a few hours. Lori returned later that evening. Kevin told his mother that I would be spending the night. Lori went into her room so we didn't get a chance to tell her what was going on. We were going to tell her first thing in the morning.

That night around midnight my father called Lori. I don't know what they conversed about, but the next day she brought me home. When we entered the house I was without fear. I was confident that this mandated reporter would act in my best interest. Upon entering my father's apartment Lori said, "I don't know what's going on!" I told her in front of my father that he was beating me bloody. I pulled up my shirt and showed her my scars. Lori gasped at my wounds. My father then outright lied!

He told Lori that I left because I wanted to be spoiled. As I attempted to rebut my father, he punched me in the face. He punched me three or four more times as I heard Lori yell, "Bullet stop! Please stop Bullet!"

I awoke to a bloody nose, lacerated jaw, cut tongue, slightly blacked eye and a splitting headache. I was face down in the living room. My father was in his room watching television. Lori was long gone and the door was locked and chained. I was unconscious for at least a minute. I was bruised and bloody, but was so happy that Lori witnessed the abuse first hand. Lori was a mandated reporter. Not only did she see my scars, but she personally witnessed a man punch his thirteen year old son unconscious.

For days I waited for the police or DCFS to knock at my father's door. For days I waited for someone to take Dexter and me out of that abusive house. But, that help never came. I guess my father referring Lori for a job bought her loyalty to him. I developed a hate for Lori that rivaled the feelings that I had towards my sister Telly. I had lost all faith in the system. I lost all faith in religion and humanity…the perfect ingredients for a murderer! I never reported my abuse again.

My relationship with my brother, Dexter, was changing for the worse. He became evidently envious of my athletic accomplishments. He played every sport I played. I thought that I was an inspiration but I later understood that he was looking for the one thing he could do better than me. The fact that he was not as athletically inclined as I was ignited his envy. You could see that it irritated him that I didn't allow my father to dominate me. He wasn't as tough or as strong willed as I was. He became envious at the fact that my father couldn't break my resolve or will, even with the eminent threat of physical abuse.

My father began to notice the separation and played my brother against it. My brother cried a lot. Because of that, our father frequently called Dexter a sissy, a pussy or a faggot. He used to tell him he needed to be tough like me. This of course made my brother hate me even worse. I could recall my brother crying to my father exclaiming that he felt my father was more proud of my accomplishments than his.

One day Tiffany came to me and exclaimed that Dexter had raped a girl. I asked her to elaborate. Tiffany went on to say that my brother was kissing on a girl and taking her clothes off. The girl realized after her panties were off that she didn't want to have sex. The girl then told Dexter that she didn't want to go any further. Tiffany went on to tell me that Dexter pinned the girl down and inserted his penis inside of her. I thought the story may have been exaggerated. Tiffany came to me on a separate occasion and told me almost the same thing happened again. I asked Dexter about the situation and he assured me it was not true. I didn't think my brother was capable of rape but I did notice how my brother treated women. He treated them like second class citizens. He dominated them like he witnessed my father doing. Dexter constantly disrespected Fran. He started to imitate my father's actions more and more.

NFL AWARDS

    Since I was good in football my father sent me to Mt. Carmel High School. They had the best football team in the state for years. The school was over 95% Caucasian. There were only a few black guys attending Mt Carmel that were not athletes. It was an all-male Catholic school. I had Donovan McNabb (quarterback for the Philadelphia Eagles) and Antoine Walker (forward for the Boston Celtics and Miami Heat) in my class. They both were really good people. I was so short that Antoine would dribble the ball between his legs and I would maneuver between his legs to try and steal the ball. Donovan McNabb had big ears. We would run past him and scream, "Ear ears!"

    I had problems from day one at Mt. Carmel. It is like a rite of passage that the freshmen suffered. One of my first days there, I was walking down the stairs to get to my class. A much bigger upper classman pushed me backwards onto my butt. I jumped up and drilled him in his face a few times. One of the teachers grabbed me and took me to the dean. I tried to explain to the Dean that I was physically assaulted, and in turn I defended myself. As punishment, I had to wash black boards after school for a few weeks. I was a regular visitor to the Dean, and not in a good way.

Since that first fight, the Dean instructed me to channel my anger and aggression. He told me to join their amateur boxing team. I took him up on his offer. I was going to knock out any opponent in the ring against me. My first opponent was a slender white guy. He was an upperclassman and a great boxer. He beat me pretty bad the first round. In the second round I was still getting beat until I threw a hay-maker. I threw the punch out of desperation and it landed. I rocked him. My opponent stumbled back and covered up. I found his Achilles heel, he couldn't handle my power. I bombarded him with a flurry of thunderous punches, but he was too skilled. He won by unanimous decision but he was wary of my power after that. That fight gave me confidence, but I was oblivious to my Achilles heel...I couldn't box.

The next guy I fought was a Hispanic guy. I saw him watching my previous fight so I knew he would be weary of my power. Boy was I wrong. That Julio Caesar Chavez looking dude beat the crap out of me! He hit me with jabs, crosses, hooks and uppercuts. I was dazed but I am pretty sure when he had me on the ropes, he climbed out of the ring, grabbed a cement block, and hit me with that too! He buzzed around the ring the whole time he beat me. How can you beat someone so bad and not get tired? He beat me so bad that by the end of the second round my corner was telling me to quit. I would never quit, plus I had just watched Rocky! I waited for my time to come to land my thunderous right cross. But my moment never came. That Hispanic dude beat me like I had just banned tacos from the school menu. I practiced a lot more and later made it to the Chicago golden gloves novice division finals.

I remember my history teacher at Mt. Carmel. He was cock eyed. He was one of the few teachers that didn't have the title 'brother', as in priest, in front of his name. He was the head basketball coach as well. He was evidently racist. One of the first days of class he was placing his students' names with their faces. The students annunciated their names and where they were from. I told him my name and he then queried, "What project are you from?" Most of the students in my class laughed. The other black kid in my class just gave me that look that said, "This muthafucka!"

I remember when we arrived to the African history part in history class. The history teacher in his Nazi fashion said, "We aren't going over that!" I very loudly asked why. The teacher replied, "Because it's not important." I can't believe someone is saying this to me! I retorted, "Why is it not important when the best players on your team originated from there?" He told me to shut up. His actions enraged me. I took my fingers like a gun and mimicked shooting him. He sent me to the office, but not before he yelled, "Like I am ever going to be driving by the projects so you and your gangbanging family would actually have a chance to shoot me!" I was sent to the Dean's office for disrupting class. The Dean was mean, but he was fair. He had a pride for his school. I respected that about him. Too bad he had a racist on his payroll. I washed so many blackboards that I felt like Daniel in the 'Karate Kid'... Wax on. Wax off.

Since I never communicated with my father he wasn't willing to help me. I needed football cleats to play. I only had gym shoes. I did well in my gym shoes but I never had a true chance to start. It was a frustrating time for me because I knew that I should have been starting. My father used to tell his friends that Mt. Carmel's racism was the reason I didn't start. That was far from the truth.

The only good thing about Mt. Carmel was that my friend from the neighborhood, Wysingo, attended the school with me. I never ate lunch at school because you had to pay for lunch. My father never asked or cared to find out how I was eating at school. I had to steal food. I would go into the line like I was buying food. When nobody was paying attention, I would grab some mozzarella sticks and put them in my pocket and walk off. Sometimes when I approached the lunch line, eyes would be on me, so I had to abandon the mozzarella plan.

I was too immature. I had little self-control or discipline. I got into too many altercations with students and teachers. My heart was filled with anger. I was too quick to react with aggression. Finally the Dean had enough. I only spent a semester at Mt. Carmel before I was told not to come back.

Every year in the late summer/early fall we would go to the NFL Awards Banquet. It was called the John Mackey Awards. John Mackey was a hall of famer tight end. NFL players from all teams would attend. All the kids would get a white football. The football was what the NFL players used to sign their autograph. Some of the cocky players would try to pry the football from my hands and sign it, whether I asked them to or not. My autograph was the only signature I wanted to see on my ball. I walked around that banquet with my ball squeezed to my chest with both hands.

    I met hall of famers John Mackey, Gayle Sears, Ronnie Lott and tons of other players. I saw my father sign some footballs for children. I used to laugh at the kids thinking, "Y'all don't know him from the NFL. I'm his son and I have never seen any film on him." I used to watch the past and present football players tell humorous pro stories. My father even added some stories when he played for the Chicago Bears. But, through all my research, I never found him on any roster for the Chicago Bears in the 1960's. He had to have played, because we attended the NFL awards every year.

    I kept in touch with a few friends from Mt. Carmel. Some were black and some were white. One of my white friends was going to come and visit me. I respectfully asked my father if it was ok. My father replied, "You not bringing any white people into my house. And you better not even think about bringing a white girl home!" My father's statement really confused me. My father was briefly in the military. My father allegedly played for the Chicago Bears. Both of those institutions at the time were predominantly white. I looked at sports teams the same as the military. Those are your brethren that you go to battle with.

    I was confused and frustrated that I could only have a certain type of friend. I asked my father to elaborate. My father yelled, "I don't do business with them and I don't trust them!" I told my father that I watched him talk to white people all the time. I told him how I watch him shake their hands at the NFL banquet. I witnessed him shaking white men's hands as well as give passionate hugs to white women who truly cared for him. I was trying to get some clarity on race and trust. I finally asked, "If you don't like someone but you smile in their face, doesn't that make you kind of a hypocrite?" My questioning must have hit a nerve with my father. He punched me in the face and cracked my front tooth. I knew what would happen if I asked certain questions. That was just my passive aggressive way of showing my father that I would be a more complete man, friend, father, and husband than he could ever be.

My father transferred me to Dunbar High School. It sat a block away from the projects. This was a rough area and school. I initially had problems there with my attire. I had the hand-me-down wardrobe from the 70's. Mt. Carmel was an all-boy school. The boys at Mt. Carmel had no pressure to look sharp or to show off for girls. I couldn't continue dressing like a bum at Dunbar. The rest of my freshman year, I kept my head down and stayed quiet. I was so embarrassed to be dressed like I was. I never got teased. But I didn't have any friends.

Summer quickly arrived and my freshman year was behind me. In the summer we would go to the YMCA on 63rd and Stony Island. One evening Wysingo, his little brother Brandon, Dexter, and I were leaving the YMCA. We had just finished playing basketball. We exited the YMCA and walked to the bus stop. While we were waiting for the bus, we noticed five guys across the street staring at us. They were all about my age. After a few minutes those guys ran over to us. When they reached us they asked where we lived. We told them 71st. One of the guys had a gun in his pants. He took his hand and held it over the gun like he was about to pull it on us.

The guy with the gun said, "I know y'all some GD's!" It's only GD's over there." "I hate GD's!" Before he could grab his gun I went after him. Wysingo then yelled, "We can all get down right now!" The guy with the gun backed up. He was scared. They all ran back to where they were hanging out. Before we knew it, they had more guys with them. These guys were way older. They had their guns out and they were running right at us. We had no choice but to retreat back into the YMCA.

I was so mad that as I entered the YMCA I was cussing. As soon as I entered the "Y" a female police officer placed me into handcuffs. She said the "Y" was a Christian organization and they would tolerate no profanity. We told her what happened and she later released me. Wysingo called his parents to pick us up. Dexter and Brandon were in shock and amazement over their big brothers' bravado. I think I was more shocked than them. I was scared but I would never let someone with a gun dictate my fate. I would rather lose my life fighting. Wysingo was scared too, but he wasn't going to just surrender his life. I couldn't believe it. Wysingo was brave. I never respected anyone like that before. I knew early on that bravery is what one did in the presence of fear. That meant Wysingo was brave as hell.

It was the summer of 1991. I was getting ready to go to summer football camp at Dunbar. I was ready to show this school my football abilities. My father purchased me some cleats so there was no holding me back. Playing football felt natural to me. I treated it like school. I knew schemes and when to properly use them. I watched cues the opposing players showed that gave away their stunts. Even though I knew my schemes, I took chances. Sometimes I was overly aggressive which caused me to play with a reckless abandon. When I was on defense, I would watch the tight end and I could tell if it was a run or pass play. When I played on the offensive side, I felt like I could score every time I had the ball. By the end of camp I was the starting free safety and tailback.

School was about to start. I had my driver's license, and I had my first car, a gremlin. That car looked like crap, but it was a car. I had a little money in my pocket because I started selling weed for guy on my block named Tony. Fran gave Dexter and me a whole lot of nice clothes. We finally had a nice wardrobe. I would sneak and buy extra clothing in addition to what Fran bought us. Everything was neatly coordinated and sharp. I entered my sophomore year at Dunbar way differently. I looked people in the eyes. I was more involved in class. My teachers liked me. I had confidence with the ladies. The girls actually were into me. I still had my individualism. I could hang with the thugs and I was just as comfortable with the nerds. I didn't have to show I was tough because I maintained a level of respect by all.

The word came back to me that the captain of the pom-pom team liked me. No way! She was way too gorgeous. She had an hour glass shape. She had long full hair. She was tiny but her breasts were huge and she had a big booty. She was a straight 'A' student and the top in her class. Her name was Tish. All the guys in the school wanted her. This had to be a rumor. She was one of the most beautiful ladies in the school. Hell! She was one of the prettiest girls in Chicago.

The pom-pom squad practiced at the same time the football team practiced. We had to walk past them to get outside. One day as I passed Tish, she looked up at me and didn't stop staring. I spoke to her and she smiled. I gathered up the courage to ask her out. We ended up dating. Lucky for me she had an affinity for bad boys. I took Tish out to nice restaurants. We would have food cooked right in front of us.

Tish would sneak me in her house and I would spend the night. One night Tish wanted to have sex with me. I rejected her. I wanted our first time to be special. Neither one of us was a virgin. But I was in love with her. Things that I did for Tish came naturally. I wrote her poems. I bought her presents for no reason. I talked on the phone with her for hours a day. I didn't want to treat her like sex was all I wanted. I wanted to marry her. It was like a movie. I was the man on my team. She was the gorgeous lady that cheered me on. I let her into my life. She knew of my abuse. She knew of me selling drugs. She knew where I kept my money. She never asked for a dime. She was used to money. She told me her last boyfriend sold crack, and made more money than I did. She left him because he had no future. Tish was still good friends with her ex. I didn't like the relationship she maintained with her ex, but I trusted her.

I was still growing. Even though the extension cords still made me bleed, I never cried. My father didn't get the satisfaction, so the extension cord beating eventually stopped. I wasn't quite eye to eye with my father. I was slightly stockier than him. He heard of my many fights on the street. My father punished me in a way that he believed kept the fear in me. Now I only got punched or slapped in the face. Nevertheless, I still brought Tish over. I loved her and she alone made my world better.

The nightmares of my mother dramatically lessened while I was with Tish. She was the only person that unconditionally put my feelings first. That meant a lot to me. Everybody in the house loved her…even my father. Since my room was in the back of the apartment, I would sneak and let her spend the night. We weren't having sex so it was easy to stay quiet. Four months later on my birthday we had sex. It was everything that I imagined it would be. Since she was a pom-pom girl, she pulled her legs back in ways unimaginable to me. She was athletic enough to hold positions that I would dare to dream. She even did the splits! I was hooked. I knew I was going to go to college and I was going to marry her.

Playing football was therapeutic for me. The guys I played with were close to me like my brothers. Our head coach was like our father…but better. The assistant coaches were like our uncles. I needed to play football like I needed to breathe. And they needed me to help them win. I still was getting abused. My teammates began to tire of the abuse. Two guys on the team were named Sam and Karlton. They both told me that if I was abused when they were around, then we would all jump my father. I still remember the one day they came over to my apartment to visit me. My father was in no mood to hide his abuse and he hit me. All three of us jumped up. My father yelled, "Oh! You got them to jump me!" The way he exclaimed seemed to be for someone else to hear. All of a sudden my father's friend rushed into our apartment and dragged him out of the house. He kept yelling like he wanted to fight us, however, his legs exited the apartment with ease. My father actually avoided me for a few days. He never brought that situation up again.

The playoffs were coming up for the sophomore football team. I had the flu so I couldn't play offense and defense. The coaches decided they needed me more on defense. I had to be assisted off the field every time the defense had to return to the sideline. I still played my heart out. I left the game with ten tackles, and four of those tackles were sacks. The coaches noticed my defensive prowess. I only played defense after that game. As we were preparing for the championship game the principal of Dunbar approached me. His name was Dr. Banks. He told me to leave Tish alone. He said that she was the top student in her class and that I was a street hood with no real future. I was taken aback by that statement. I went to Tish and told her what our principal just told me. She said that Dr. Banks was attracted to her mom and acted like she was his daughter. Dr. Banks also went to Tish's mom and told her mom that I was a sadistic street thug with an affinity for hurting football players on the field.

Much to the dismay of our principal, I still dated Tish. One day before practice I was kissing Tish in the hallway. That kiss made me a few seconds late to practice. Dr. Banks went to my coach and told him that I was late to practice because I was kissing Tish. He then had my coach suspend me for the next game for being late. I missed the championship game. That killed me on the inside. I let my team down. I should have been there for them; instead my actions lead to a one game suspension. I got really depressed. If Dunbar didn't have metal detectors I would have brought my revolver to school and shot the principal in his office. I had never felt that way before. I couldn't control my feelings. I knew if I saw him I would shoot him. I never understood an adult male that used his power to hurt or abuse children. He was no different than my father.

Our football season was over. In the wake of my absence, we lost. I decided I would join the wrestling team. This was another activity that would keep me away from home. I worked my way up on the wrestling team. I became one of the best 125 pound wrestlers in the city. We went all over the nation wrestling in tournaments. I only lost two matches all year. Both losses were to ranked opponents. I ended up tearing cartilage in my left knee, in the quarterfinals of the city tournament. I couldn't continue because I had to have an operation. I was on crutches for a while, but that didn't bother me. Wrestling was something to do to stay out of the house. I really didn't like it.

I was close with all of my teammates at Dunbar. But I hung with one more than others. He was our middle linebacker. We called him Poodle. He was about six feet tall and weighed about 200 pounds. He was the hardest hitter on our team. He called the formations and knew his position well. He rarely smiled and he let his actions on the field do all of the talking. We went everywhere together. He knew of the abuse suffered by my father. He allowed me to stay with him and his grandmother on many occasions. I loved him like a brother. We were tight like brothers too. His only downfall was his insecurity. He told me that one of his friends slept with a girl he was dating. This act manifested itself by causing him to not fully trust his friends. He used to tell me to not be as friendly with his girlfriends because it made him feel uncomfortable. That was a hard thing for me to do. I was loyal to a fault. I could never betray a friend's trust. I looked at him like a brother, so I naturally treated his girlfriends like my sisters. In later years that would come to bite me in the ass.

HOME LESS

It was almost Thanksgiving, but I was about to have little reason for thanks. Tish called me on the phone. She sounded different. After an hour of babbling about nothing, Tish finally told me that she was drinking with her ex. She claimed that she became drunk and had sex with him. I couldn't believe my ears. I laughed it off, like it didn't bother me, but it killed me. Tish would always tell me that her ex still wanted to be with her. I always told her the situation made me feel uncomfortable. She assured me, however, that there was no chance for intimacy between them. That incident blew out my only candle that had shown light and warmth on humanity. Tish encompassed all that I believed was good in this world…beauty, virtue, honesty, integrity, loyalty, commitment, passion, excitement, and most of all love.

My world came crumbling down. I lost all trust in women. As a matter of fact I hated women. Maybe they are all like Telly, Lori, and Tish. Maybe that is why my father beat them. I wasn't confused. I was with a new resolve…a resolve to never be vulnerable again. I wouldn't allow myself to become vulnerable to another woman. I was going to hurt them before they hurt me. Most of all, I would never fall in love again. I needed to get away. I continued to date Tish, but it was never the same. She tried real hard to rectify the situation, but my heart was no longer hers. Between my principal harassing me and the infidelities of my girlfriend, I had to leave Dunbar High School.

It was late fall of my sophomore year in high school. The Chicago cold was already present. I returned home from school to hear my father yelling at Terrance. My father was upset that Terrance was eating the fried chicken that he had bought for the family. My father believed since Terrance avoided him, then Terrance didn't have the right to each the food he bought. Terrance truly hated my father. Terrance didn't respect the way my father treated his mom or us. Every time my father yelled at Terrance, he would defiantly click his teeth, smack his lips, or reply under his breath "whatever". While my father was yelling at Terrance over the chicken, Terrance kept smacking his lips.

Terrance's antics upset my father so bad that he called me in the kitchen to beat up Terrance. I laughed at my father. I would have been more likely to jump on him. This reaction upset my dad even more. He then yelled for my sycophant brother to fight Terrance. Fran knew how Dexter was so she immediately yelled, "No!" Dexter jumped up and aggressively walked towards Terrance. Just before he reached Terrance, Dexter yelled, "Don't mess with my daddy!" Fran jumped in the middle and kept them apart.

Immediately after the altercation my father overheard Tiffany, Terrance, and myself laughing together. Since my father was upset, he expected everyone in the house to be on edge. The fact that we were having fun infuriated my father. He stormed into the living room where we were playing. My father looked at me and said, "Since you hate it here, leave!" I didn't even look at him. He was mad that I didn't fight his fight. He was mad that I made him look childish by not stooping to his level. He was really mad that he couldn't instill fear in me.

Every day I came home from school my father would ask me, "Did you find somewhere to live yet?" Every day I would withhold my response and go to my room. This lasted for about two weeks. Once again Tiffany, Terrance and I were laughing while I was doing my homework. My father was obviously annoyed that day. My laughter was probably the catalyst that set him off. He came into the living room where I was doing my homework. My father then asked, "Didn't I tell you to leave?" I never picked my head up. I wasn't selling weed anymore and I didn't have anywhere else to go. My father then rolled his ring to the position where the jewel of the ring sat underneath the palm of his hand. He slapped me in my face, with the jewel of his ring striking me first. I saw stars immediately. I jumped to my feet and the motion knocked the chair from under me. He knew that he couldn't beat me. I boxed, wrestled, and trained my whole life for this moment. I was going to beat him to death!

My father put his dukes up yelling, "Come on…Come on!" This time his antics of intimidation didn't work. I positioned myself in a boxing stance and Fran immediately jumped in the middle. She begged me to be the bigger man and leave. My father yelled, "Get out of my house!" He then told me, "In a few weeks you will be sixteen. You are big enough to where I don't know if I can take you. But you are old enough to where if you come back into my house I can blow you fucking head off!" As I walked to my room to get my things Tiffany exclaimed, "You can't do that!" My father turned to her and said, "You get out of my house, too!"

While I was packing, my father came into my room and told me not to take anything that Fran bought me. He told me that she only bought me those clothes because of him, therefore they belonged to him. If those clothes weren't so nice I would have given them back. I continued to pack all my clothes staring him right in the face. He knew not to approach me. He knew that I was taking all my clothes. My gun was a few feet away from me, but I didn't need it. My father couldn't beat me if he tried. And, I was getting what I wanted…to be away from my abusive, tyrant of a father.

Fran called her friend who was out of town and asked if we could stay in her apartment. Fran's friend allowed me and my eleven year old step sister to stay at her house, while she was on vacation. We were only there a few days when Tiffany started crying. The problem was that Tiffany never stopped crying. She cried so much that I knew something was wrong. I knew this was more than feelings. I knew this was a mental breakdown. I called Fran and told her that Tiffany wouldn't stop crying. Fran told me Tiffany could come back if she apologized to my father.

Fran came to get Tiffany. Tiffany apologized to my father and was allowed to move back in. I had to be out of her friend's apartment in a few days. She would be returning from vacation soon. A few days later I was homeless. I slept in the warm stairwells of apartment buildings. I had to be careful to look like I was waiting on someone, when people were on the stairs. I had to master sleeping for minutes at a time. A week after that, I turned sixteen. What a way to celebrate my sixteenth birthday…as a homeless teen.

    I bounced from friend's houses as much as I could. But, times were hard and parents couldn't afford to feed another mouth. It was the winter so I learned the tricks fast…if you want to stay warm, you go to the public library. The problem with the library is if you fall asleep, they would ask you to leave. After getting put out a few times in the winter, I made sure I was reading…or faking it damn good. More times than not, I had to stay woke and read because the librarians patrolled often. I spent months as a vagrant in the library near 74th and Jeffery. I literally read book after book. I questioned religion so I read on topics spanning from Catholicism to Buddhism. I read biographies and books on world history. I didn't know it at the time, but reading all those books helped my articulation and overall ability to excel in school.

    A well-seasoned homeless man told me about a grate in the ground near down town Chicago. It was right by Randolph Street. In the winter if you stood on the grating you would be warmed by the exiting steam. It didn't matter how cold it got, the hot air coming from that grating would keep you warm. The problem was that the police always kicked the homeless people away from that spot.

    My mom had a brother and sister. I often wondered why they didn't make sure their nephews were ok. They all knew of my father beating my mom. They all knew he was abusive. The feeling of having nobody on my side was the final catalyst that allowed me to transform into America's nightmare. I lost respect for God; love; and I lost the true value of human life. I ended up committing some truly heinous and unforgiveable crimes.

    I was completely destitute. I lost weight from a lack of eating. I became very proficient at stealing cereal from a grocery store on 71st and Exchange. I would wear baggy clothes and put the box under my shirt. I would squeeze the box until it "popped". Squeezing the air out collapsed the box to a much smaller size, which made it easier to smuggle out of the store. I would go somewhere and eat the sugar laden cereal and use tap water instead of milk. I hated it at first, but it was something to eat. Later, I became so accustomed to eating cereal with water that I only wanted it that way. I continued to eat cereal with water until my late twenties.

To bring in some money, I became a lookout for a local drug dealer named Mike. He used to keep youngsters around him. Mike would pay youngsters to do odd jobs or to watch out for the police. He used to give the kids free food and candy as long as they begged. I never begged, so I had to earn mine. It was a cold day in January. A few of us broke kids went to Mike's house in the morning to see if he had work. I will never forget what happened next. Mike was eating a sausage biscuit. We were hungry and destitute. We were used to Mike giving up his scraps so we patiently waited. The younger teen who was with me begged him for a sausage biscuit. Mike replied, "If y'all want a biscuit, y'all going to have to suck my dick!" I laughed. My laughter quickly died down because the look on Mike's face was serious. Mike wasn't joking at all.

The teen asked again only to receive the same response from Mike. The boy started crying and continued begging for a sandwich. Mike walked up to the teen and pulled his dick out. He grabbed the crying teen by his shoulder and pulled him to the corner of his living room. The boy kept crying and pleading. Mike and the boy continued to talk, but I couldn't hear their conversation. The boy must not have been satisfied with what he was hearing because he continued to sob quietly. They conversed back and forth for a few minutes. Finally I heard Mike say, "Fuck it! You ain't gonna get shit then!" I heard the teen say, "Okay, Okay!" Then the teen allowed Mike to push him to his knees. Mike then pointed his penis in the boy's facial area. I stood there in disbelief. Was Mike gay? Was the other boy gay? How many times had they done this? Are those breakfast sandwiches that damned good?

I was snapped out of my haze by Mike's voice sternly directing the boy to "Do it like you're supposed to!" I now was fully focused. My inner turmoil turned from astonishment, to rage, to murderous intentions. I wanted to kill Mike. I never had that feeling for anyone other than my father, but it was undeniable. I never had this deep of a wanting to kill someone…not even my father. But that rage turned into a realization that the boy participated as well. He was not forced. He could have said no…like I never had to. I left the house and never interacted with Mike again.

    I washed up in the sinks at school, and at the library. I hid the problem pretty well for a while. I needed money so I started robbing the low level dealers. I robbed a few acquaintances of mine that I knew had money. I would drive around looking for "corner boys" that weren't paying too much attention to their surroundings. I would drive four or five blocks down and then creep back jumping fences and taking alley ways. I would creep up on the guys and put the revolver to one of their heads. I would only rob one or two dealers at a time. I worked alone and it would be suicide to try to rob three or more people. These guys were killers, but they were cowards. They couldn't fight and a gun to their heads made them give up totally. I would rob them for their jewelry, money, pagers, burner cellphones, marijuana, and dope. Contrary to popular folk tales, you cannot get rich robbing street corner dealers. The only thing you are almost guaranteed to get is killed.

    I remember robbing this one man. He was in his mid to late twenties. I parked my car four blocks down on a side street. I had to stay in the shadows. I jumped fences and used the darkness of the alley to creep behind him. I shoved the gun in his lower back and told him to, "Empty your fucking pockets!" He responded by whipping around and stabbing me in my left side with a knife. I stumbled back, gasping to catch my breath. Before I could regroup, the man came back at me with the blade. He was about to stab me again.

    I fired, hitting him twice in the chest. This was the first time I had shot someone. It was either me or him. When a person gets shot, it is nothing like in the movies. People don't fall coordinated or gracefully, but rather flop clumsily to the ground. The first thing they do is beg for you not to kill them. The blood doesn't run neatly into the streets. It initially rushes out; until it saturates every part of clothing it touches. The victim's breathing is not regular. Every breath is forced and painful. It seemed as if every breath was hastened and devoid of a natural rhythm.

Out of fear of getting spotted I immediately retreated, leaving the man to lie in his own blood. As I ran away I could hear the man faintly screaming, "Help me! Help me!" I didn't get a dime from the man. I was out of breath from the knife that was just inserted into my left ribcage. I was in too much pain to run. I pressed the stab wound with my left hand, in an attempt to slow the bleeding, as I painfully jogged to the car. The scene would give the toughest man nightmares, but I wasn't a man, I was another psycho raised on the Chicago streets.

Days afterward, the stab wound became seriously infected. The wound started oozing puss and began to really stink. The pain was unbearable. It hurt to breath. I couldn't go to the hospital out of fear of getting linked to the shooting in the alley. I became sick for almost a month. My wound needed stitches, but I knew I couldn't go to a hospital. I kept wrapping it with gauze to keep the laceration closed. I could feel my heartbeat in the wound. Painkillers and ointment that I stole from the store did little to help, but the cut eventually healed into an ugly scar along my left ribs.

I never intended to shoot the man in the alley. It didn't bother me that I had to. I constantly told myself, "He was breathing when I left him, so he had to be alive." This wasn't the life I chose. I didn't ask to be born. God gave me my terrible parents. God was the one who allowed me to be born in Hell. Since I was born in Hell, God has no right to be upset that I adjusted so well to the fire!

I started to hear rumors that I was the guy robbing the corner boys. A couple of dealers even asked me if I was committing the robberies. I looked them straight in the eye and denied it. I attempted to rob two men selling crack near 71st. I thought I caught them by surprise. I tried to sneak up, but as I approached they turned around and started shooting at me! It was like they knew I was coming. Better yet, it was like they had eyes in the back of their heads.

I crotched low, ran to a side of a metal dumpster, and started shooting back. Now they are calling for backup. Men started running out of the apartment above them. They were shooting at me as well. I ran out of bullets. I knew I was going to die that night. The only thing that saved me was their hesitation. For whatever reason, they continued to shoot at me from across the alley. They probably didn't know I had run out of bullets. While they were sending bullet after bullet in my direction, I stayed low and ran. In my haste I dropped my damn revolver. I couldn't rob anyone without a gun. What was I going to do if I got cornered by guys with guns…throw rocks at them?

    Now I am really broke. I am starting to stink from the inability to take baths on a regular. I would walk into McDonalds and wash up their sink, but I had to put back on the same smelly clothes that I barely washed. My friend's mom let me keep my clothes at her house, but I was too embarrassed to get a change of clothes from her. It was so cold that I rode the bus for hours to stay warm. I would ride until the end and then ride it back again. I never knew about shelters or anything of the sort. I am glad I didn't because I needed to suffer…to find myself. I was walking past a demolished building and picked up a small plumbing pipe. It was about ¾ inch in diameter and about twelve inches long. I could hide it easily in my sleeve and pull it out if I had to use it.

    I kept that pipe in my coat. I could push the end of the pipe against the inside of my coat to resemble a gun. Most people wouldn't have the guts to call my bluff. I robbed a few people on the Chicago Transit Authority with that piece of metal. Out of desperation, I robbed a corner dealer with that pipe. He had around $440 and a scratched up 380 semi-automatic pistol. Now that I have a gun, I am back in business.

    I recall I was on the CTA in the winter. I was just riding to stay out of the cold. I should have been in school, but I was too cold, too broke, and too smelly to go. A boy my age was sitting with a group of his peers on the back of the city bus. The bus we were on let me know he attended Chicago's High School for Agricultural Science.

    The boy kept staring me down with his hat turned to the left. He was well groomed and you could tell well taken care of at home. I immediately got upset. I kept saying to myself, "This nigga probably has both parents at home but wants to portray street life!" I lived the street life and I abhorred it! Anybody who lived in the streets knew it was nothing to glorify. It might seem as if we glorify street life, but it is more of a coping mechanism. I remember having multiple conversations with guys talking about what we could have become if we would have had good parents. Anyway…back to the bus ride.

I walked to the back of the bus and sat right next to this pretend thug. The mean looks he was giving me quickly disappeared. I asked him if he was a Black Stone. He said no and straightened his hat to the front. I pulled out my gun and shoved it into his ribs. The people with him instantly moved one seat away from him on all sides. He put his hands up and I harshly whispered, "Put you goddamn hands down before I kill you!" He was scared shitless and immediately put his hands down. I took his money, his bus tokens, his hat, and his brand new ¾ length leather jacket. I would have taken his Nikes, but they didn't fit me.

Before I left, I apologized to one of the cute girls with him, for my actions. She smiled and replied, "Oh that's ok!" The way she acted caused me to like her. You could tell she liked bad boys. I would have asked for her phone number, but I knew the police would have been after me. As soon as the bus stopped at Chicago High School for Agricultural Science, he and his friends ran off the bus. They kept running. I knew they were running to get help and to report the robbery.

I also started stealing cars for money. I stole cars like Deltas or 88's or any similar short-bodied car. These short-bodied cars had a small triangular window in the back. All I had to do was break out that small window to gain access to the back seat. That window was so small that cops wouldn't notice the glass was broken. I would then reach through that window and unlock the back door and work my way up to the front. Next, I used a screwdriver to tear the plastic from the steering column. Tearing the plastic off exposed the ignition pin. After having the ignition pin exposed, I used the screwdriver to push the pin to start the ignition. I could literally steal a car in less than four minutes.

I would go to the suburbs to steal the cars because it was less likely that Chicago PD would be looking for them. Before I pulled off, I would make sure all the signal lights functioned properly, and that the tags were up to date. Not checking for the small things was a sure way to get pulled over. I never had more than one guy in the car so that the cops wouldn't focus on us or decide to run the license plate number. Everyone knew where the chop shops were. The tricky part was getting the proper reference so they would take your car. You can't just take a stolen car to a chop shop if they don't know you.

    Even though I was homeless, my athletic achievements were pouring in. My junior year I became one the captains on the football and wrestling team. The best players in the city were invited to a Chicago Bears camp. Needless to say I was present during that camp. During that year the Chicago Public Schools were having problems with funding their athletic programs. I was one of two people to be a spokesperson for the Chicago public school system. I was interviewed by the local news station. I was very proud to be on television.

    I loved playing football at Gately Stadium in front of all those people. They all knew who I was. They loved the way I hit. They all cheered when I returned punts. I had the respect of opposing players as well.

    A few teachers at Dunbar would pay me $25-$50 a piece after every game. The defensive back coach allowed me to call the backfield stunts and formations. If he called in a specific formation, he allowed me to change the formation if I felt differently. I was truly a student of the game. I was known for being a hard hitter. I left a receiver injured on the sidelines almost every game. I was a little terror on the field, so Coach Johnson started calling me Chucky. He got the name from that little doll that killed people in the movies. My team ended up going to the playoffs and losing in the second round. I had recruitment letters from all over. Everyday my coach would hand me letters to take home.

    Because of my absenteeism at Dunbar, people started pressuring my father about my wellbeing. To save face, my father sent word for me to contact him. After reluctantly calling my father, he told me that I couldn't move back in but my actions were bringing unwanted attention to him. I told my father that I only needed one thing from him. I needed him to transfer me from Dunbar. I had to get away from Tish and that principal. My father put on a friendly face and helped me transfer.

GANG AFFILIATED

Arriving at Simeon High School was like getting a "new lease on life". Nobody knew me. I didn't have those old demons staring me in my face. I also used the transfer to end my relationship with Tish. The coaches were elated to have a player of my caliber on their team. I only bonded with a few people in Simeon. I still hung out with Poodle, the middle linebacker from Dunbar. I occasionally stayed with him and his grandmother. Women were coming from everywhere. It was exciting to them because I was the new guy. My hygiene still wasn't the best. I was able to shower more because we worked out in the offseason. I took showers every day after practice. I received free lunch, so I was guaranteed one solid meal. I still ate stolen cereal and water almost every night.

I started hanging out with the quarterback on Simeon's football team. He stood over six feet. He was hard as nails and had a riffle for an arm. I liked him. He was tough for a quarterback. We called him Dee. I started hanging out with Dee a lot. Dee was a member of the Chicago gang, Black Disciples. He thought I was tough and asked me if I wanted to be one too. I figured becoming a BD was a good financial opportunity for me. They were known for raking in money from drug sales. I could sell some drugs and get out of this poverty. Plus all of his people were BD's. During this time there was an outright war between the BD's and the GD's. If we got caught by any GD's they were going to kill me simply because of association.

I became a member with BD organization. It was sort of generic how easy it was for me to become a member. Dee brought me to the "Minister" of the BD's and I stood in front of him. Dee told the "Minister" that he vouched for me. The "Minister" asked if I had been plugged in any other organization and I responded in the negative. The "Minister" then pulled out a piece of paper. On the paper was the Black Disciples' prayer and creed. It puzzled me that the minister hadn't committed the prayer to memory. Even with the paper, the minister stumbled through the prayer. Then he would pause to give me a chance to repeat the recited words. After bumbling through the prayer I had to recite the creed. I was taught the handshake and given several pieces of papers. The papers contained BD literature for me to memorize. All the BD's rushed in to welcome their newest member by performing the BD handshake with me. I was officially a Black Disciple.

The word spread fast that I became a BD. It shocked a lot of people because I hung out with a lot GD's. Word even got back to the home I was ostracized from. I remember Tiffany calling me and asking me if it was true. I told her yes but she in turn just accused me of lying. I was teaming with pride filled affiliation, so I took Dexter, Tiffany, and Terrance to my set on 119th and Princeton. All of the BD's (most of which were rough looking men in the twenties and thirties) came out to greet me with the BD handshake. My siblings couldn't believe it. They were just as excited as I was. Tiffany and Dexter started throwing up the BD sign with their three fingers high in the air. Some of the guys came up to the car and told my siblings that if they ever have any problems at home to call. They were told that we were a family now. Word spread quickly to my father. I knew it would. With a newfound sense of pride and defiance, I started visiting my siblings at my father's house. I visited often. At times

I brought some of the BD's with me. Sometimes I was even brazen enough to stay all night.

I respected my father. The guys with me respected him as well. My father's fear of what we were capable of really humbled him. I still disliked my father, but I got more pleasure out of watching him tiptoe around me. I thought Dexter would finally become an individual now because he knew I could protect him by myself, and with my deadly crew. Much to my dismay, my brother really didn't change. He still felt the need to kiss his father's ass to feel safe. He still disliked anyone other than himself that was close to our father. The only change in my brother was that he walked around pretending he was a BD.

True gang life started immediately after I became a BD. I was involved in a gang fight or shooting almost every week. I started staying with Dee and his father. We were robbing people on a daily. We would go to school, go to football practice, and then rob people for money. We rarely robbed people together. But we would share our tales often. We would go to schools like Whitney Young, where girls had a prominent future. We would have sex with these girls and rob them for everything we could stuff in our pockets. They were into stealing cars, so I started back, too. We would drive to the suburbs and steal cars. After we stole the cars, we would take them to known "chop shops", but none of us had connections to deal with them. We pulled up to the chop shops with five or six short body cars, just to be told to leave.

I remember it was the summer of my seventeenth birthday. We had just stolen four cars from Lincoln Park. We were driving near 63rd street when I passed two policemen in a marked squad car. They were in front of me going the opposite direction. We both came to a two way stop sign. They reached their stop before I did, so they stopped and waited. Before I came to a complete stop, I noticed that they were staring right at me. Did they run the plates that fast? Why were they looking at me so hard? In my state of paranoia, I performed a rolling stop, in an effort to be able to speed off faster. Before I completed my rolling stop, the police lady who was driving pointed with her finger, motioning for me to pull over. I was scared out of my mind. As soon as she pointed, I floored the gas pedal and was at least a few blocks down. I looked in my rear view and noticed that the driver was having problems performing her 180 degree turn. I sped down two more streets and made a frantic left hand turn.

As soon as I could, I jumped out of the moving car and hit the street running. I threw off my shirt and continued running. I almost knocked over a little boy turning the corner of an adjacent building. I stopped him from falling and asked, "Are there any cops behind me?" He took a hard stare and said, "Nope!" I raced around him and ran to an empty lot across the street. The empty lot had tall, brown weeds in it. I heard sirens but I never lifted my head to see where they were. I stayed in those weeds for hours. Bugs and ants were biting at my exposed torso, but my fear of being arrested kept me from moving. We were supposed to be stealing cars for money, but it ended up being just joy rides most of the time. After that incident, I never stole another car again.

We went all over the city hanging out with BD's from other cliques. I got to know a lot of guys. Some were true soldiers that did what was asked of them unconditionally. Some were straight killers. Some were cowards. I never identified with any of them. Most of them were tough only when they had the numbers or a gun. Most of them were somewhat loyal to the organization, but they stood for nothing else. I was fearless with or without a gun…with or without my crew. Dee and I used to go to other sets and help out with fights or problems. We would beat people so bad that BD's in the 100's nicknamed us 'Bone Crushers'. I was immersing in the gang life more and more. I loved the thirty on thirty fights in the street. I wanted things to go wrong so I could start shooting. School was no longer a learning ground for me, but a place to resonate my gang affiliation.

I was constantly suspended for fights and gang banging. The fact that the gang war in Chicago had escalated didn't bother me. I didn't mind having to watch my back. I loved knowing that I might have to start shooting at any moment. I got a rush off of the excitement, like an adrenaline junky. If it wasn't for eligibility requirements to play football, I would have never gone to school. I was arrested several times during this period. The only thing that saved me was that I was a known football player in Chicago. Cops would always tell me to get my life together and that I had a future. They would tell me a conviction would hurt me, so a lot of times they would let me go.

Dexter called me out of the blue to tell me that Telly and the kids came up to visit. He told me to stop by and say hello. I could give two cents about Telly but I loved my niece and nephew. I took Dee along with me, to be my excuse, when I was ready to leave. When we arrived at my father's apartment, I hugged my niece and nephew. It was so nice to see them. They were loving and hilariously country. My niece seemed better. She was pleasant. I didn't feel uncomfortable around her.

Within an hour of being there, another BD called and said he knew some girls who wanted to hookup. Telly let us use her car. Dexter also came with us. We picked another BD and headed to see the girls. My friends were pleased to find several women in the house. Unfortunately, there were several kids in the house as well. I didn't like any of the girls there. They seemed really low class. My guys were into the fast girls, but I was fine not hooking up with anyone.

Being in a house full of bug-a-boos was an instant mood killer. All I wanted to do was sit until it was time to leave. The woman who lived in the house asked me to take her to the liquor store. I told her no. She said if I allowed her to drive quickly to the liquor store, she would fill the gas tank up. I had to fill the tank before I got home so I agreed.

An hour went past and the lady had yet to return. Another hour went past. We were starting to get weary. One of the girl's friends stated, "You should have never let her use your car! She is not coming back!" I kind of chuckled only to realize that she was not joking. It started getting late. Most of the visitors went home. My brother, Dee, another BD, and I were in a house with the stowaway's kids. We impatiently waited. She had to come back, her kids were there.

Night turned to day. This bitch still hasn't come home! We all gathered on her front porch to contemplate what to do next. While we were going over our next move, the lady drove past in my sister's car. She was looking to see if we were still at her house. I darted after the car, but she sped off.

We were in hostile gang territory with no weapons and no vehicle. I was beyond pissed. I ran into the house. Two of her children were under four. The other two children appeared to be five and six years of age. I was uncontrollably angry. I told my guys the plan, "We kill her kids one by one until she brings back the car! When she finally gets here, we kill her too!"

Dexter was scared. Dee started to laugh because he thought I was just venting. I exclaimed, "I will throw her kids out of this second story window onto the fucking concrete!" I snatched her smallest child by his foot and carried him to the window. Dexter screamed, "No! No! You can't kill her kids!" Dee snatched the crying child from my hand and placed the excrement ridden toddler back on the floor.

I was morphing into an emotionally driven gang banger with an appetite for revenge. Whatever innocence I possessed was gone. I was destined for Hell. I was sliding down a gasoline slide, smoking a cigarette, while holding two grenades!

Dee yelled, "She doesn't even care about her own kids!" As I thought about it, I knew she didn't. She left her four toddlers alone, with strangers for two days, without changing them or giving them food or water. For all she knew, her kids could have been dead already.

My father had been paging me for over a day. I had to call him. I had my little brother with me. I called my father from a phone in the house. My father yelled, "You better not have my son in none of your bullshit!" I explained the whole situation. My father called the cops to report my sister's car being stolen. The police pulled over the lady in my sister's car hours later. She escaped being arrested by telling the police that I allowed her to drive the car for sex. I hated my sister so it really humbled me to have to explain the whole situation.

Dee and I got ready to go back to his father's apartment. I drove my sister's car and Dee was riding shotgun. My nephew, my sister Telly, and Dexter were in the back seat. While we were parking in Dee's father's complex, the local dope dealer and his lady walked past the car. My three year old nephew was staring at the dope dealer's beautiful girlfriend.

The dealer yelled at my nephew, "What the hell are you staring at?" I responded through an open window, "He is only three. He can look at whatever he wants!" The dealer replied, "Say that shit again?" I snapped back, "You heard me nigga!" He pulled out his semi-automatic pistol and pointed it at me. He then said, "What you got to say now?" I jumped out of the car and yelled, "You better kill me nigga! That gun doesn't change shit!" My reaction scared his girlfriend who pleaded for him to leave. I laughed and called the BD's from inside Dee's house. They came out but they knew it was too many people outside to start shooting. The dealer became frightened and left. My vengeful anger took control of me. I pondered and plotted the different scenarios of the next time the dealer and I would cross paths.

I had dreams of tying him and his girlfriend up, dousing them with gasoline, and lighting them on fire. I stalked out the guy's car and apartment for over a month. He was onto me. I barely saw him, and when I did he had a crowd with him. The opportunity to get my new adversary never arose. My overweight, ass kissing sister raced to tell my father the details of what transpired. She told my father that I had a death wish. She made it seem like I instigated the whole argument. I was sticking up for her son. I didn't know what was going on with me, but I knew I was losing control of whatever it was.

In school, all the BD foot soldiers followed me. I don't know how, but one day I looked up and they were waiting on me to give an order. Most of the time I never gave orders, I would fight myself. I started living for the reaction of fear from people who weren't BD's. I felt like a king…a poor king, but a king nonetheless. I would beat up or shoot at a rival just to hear the frantic screams of women. I had become an addict to the chaotic street life.

I was a pessimistic, self-fulfilling prophecy. People saw me as a deadly force, so I tried even harder to show how deadly I was. A BD decided to leave our organization and become a GD. He was a low level coward, so nobody cared that he left. I was so into being a BD that I took it upon myself to teach him a lesson. The next morning, I brought my gun to school to kill him. When I saw him get off the city bus, I walked over to intercept him by the front of the school.

I pulled out my gun and rushed towards him. The other BD's followed aggressively behind me. A girl, who was a mutual friend of both of us, saw what was about to happen. She quickly turned to him and yelled for him to run. He ran, and to his luck, another city bus was waiting at the stop. He got on the bus and retained his life. The crazy part about it was that nobody gave an order to kill him. To this day I don't know why I took it upon myself to exact punishment.

LIL YUMMY

We used to hang with the BD's on 108th. We called them the BD's from the '8-Ball'. I liked them over some of the other sets because they were true killers. They were reckless, abandoned, and ruthless. We would sit on the porch and talk trash, while a couple of the members would check the cars driving past. Another guy would be extra security on the porch, holding a tech-nine submachine gun. He would sit on the porch; while he watched his fellow BD's check oncoming traffic for rival gang members. The two guys stopping traffic would literally be in the street holding up traffic. They were both armed with semi-automatic pistols looking into each car. They were doing so to make sure that the oncoming vehicles didn't have GD's attempting a drive by. We were going back and forth shooting at the GD's who were housed in a building about two blocks away.

The BD's on 108th had one member who I remember all too well. He was nine years old. He shot first and asked questions later. His name was Robert Sandifer. We called him Lil' Yummy. When I first met him I was a little disappointed. I couldn't believe that men older than me would allow a kid to hang with them. I remember jokingly telling Yummy to go to school. I never met his parents. Yummy lived with and was raised by his grandparents. They loved him.

Yummy would shoot someone at the drop of a hat. But this same kid hid like a little girl when his grandparents came looking for him. Yummy's grandparents would drive around for hours trying to keep him out of trouble. The BD's would lie to his grandparents and tell them that he was never there. All the while, Yummy would be hiding in the house. They were guilty of lying, but I was just as guilty, because I said nothing.

Before a shootout, the Minister of the 108th set would constantly repeat to us, "Think like a killer!" And that is what Yummy became. Yummy would sometimes help with checking traffic for GD's. I could only imagine the fear that the citizens felt while being stopped by armed men looking into their cars.

I remember a working class man was riding in a van. We stopped the van and the minister visually searched the interior of the vehicle for possible shooters. Yummy was approaching the van at the same time the minister was waving the van to drive on. Yummy raised his right hand and threw up his middle three fingers while yelling, "BD!" The man in the van kept his eyes on the road and continued to drive. Yummy followed the van, threw up his middle three fingers, and again yelled, "BD!" The man continued to drive with his eyes stuck to the road. Yummy became upset that after two attempts, the gentleman driving the van didn't yell BD back to him. Yummy pulled out his revolver and aimed it at the man's head. The minister yelled, "Somebody get the damned gun from Yummy!"

The BD's had irreversibly ruined Yummy. He had a home. He had both grandparents to raise him. This was not cool. Everyone would brag about how deadly Yummy was. It really bothered me that we were using this little boy. Yummy never had a chance.

It was the summer of 1993. Dee and I had just arrived on the '8 Ball' set from football practice. The BD's started piling into cars with Molotov cocktails. They were about to retaliate for a drive-by performed by the GD's a few days prior. They were going to fire bomb the house and shoot anyone who ran outside. All the while, the minister was continually yelling, "Think like a killer!" They piled into two cars and drove to the GD's building. Several of us sat on the porch and waited. Within seconds I heard continuous gunfire. The BD's hastily returned.

The minister frantically jumped out of the car. He was patting out a fire on his arm. At the same time the Minister was yelling at Yummy, "How in the hell did you drop your gun?" Yummy had been frightened by the GD's return gunfire. In the aftermath, he dropped his gun. That is when I realized that he was truly a kid. He was too young to fully understand his actions. Yummy was simply following our lead. I lost respect for the killers from the '8 Ball' set. I didn't hang with them anymore.

After football practice, we would drink and talk about girls. They all smoked weed, but I could never bring myself to use any drugs or inhale any smoke. I was drinking heavily. The BD's I hung with were losers. Most of them never cared for me. They never said much because they were scared to get into a physical altercation. Dee was taller and bigger than I was. He was more like them, so they sided with him. They always tried to instigate a fight between us all the time.

Sometimes Dee and the other BD's would act like they were going to fight me. If I wasn't staying with Dee, we would have fought. I knew he wasn't a true friend, but it was so nice to have a warm place to lay my head. I decided not to live with him and his father anymore. I couldn't trust him. He was only cool when he needed my help. Plus, I had my own crew of BD's that I hung around with. I started to learn the true notion of street life…everyone for self.

DEADLY STREETS

      I started selling weed for another low level dealer. I can't recall his name, but he was a BD as well. He gave me weed on consignment and taxed me for the profit. I was barely making money, so he gave me some crack to sell. After I paid what I owed back, I still barely had any money. I was so broke that I went back to what I did best…robbery. When drug addicts came to buy crack, I would just rob them. They were fiends. Who could they tell? I made a little money off of it. But, all of a sudden, fiends stop trying to buy from our block. After almost a complete halt in drug sales, I was informed that I was "burning up the block". I was ordered to cease what I was doing or face a violation.

      There was this female fiend that used to come around and buy crack. I can't recall her name, but she had a toddler named Justin. I hated serving her when she had Justin with her. Her son was a very handsome and vibrant. Justin was really light skinned, with curly brown hair and green eyes. He was too young to walk, but he smiled all the time. I sold to her so much that Justin would lean over into my arms. I would often carry him and baby talk with him.

Seeing that I had a bond with her son, she told me about some guys that I would be able to rob easy. I told her if it pays off, I would give her a free crack rock. Justin's mom told me that it was two guys living in the basement of an abandoned house. She said she smoked dope in the basement with the guys. She told me that it was only one way in and one way out. They were both low level dealers that smoked crack. Justin's mom assured me that the two skinny guys would be an easy hit. She gave me what time to come to catch them both.

    I went to the abandoned house and they were there just like she told me. The basement door was open with no screen door. Somehow they had electricity in the basement. I saw light from a lamp and heard a stereo playing. As I walked down the stairs, I ran into a lady. She was attempting to walk up the stairs to exit the basement. I put my gun in her face and motioned with the gun to walk back into the basement.

    The woman kept her head down and never looked me in my face. She evidently knew the rules of robbery…if she doesn't see anything; she can't tell anything! She walked to the back of the basement where both men were sitting on a couch smoking weed. She sat on the couch with them and kept her head down the entire time. The fiend warned me that they had a gun so I had to make my presence known. I aggressively told the men to 'empty their pockets'. They both looked at each other in a way that I knew they were communicating without talking. I ran over and hit the bigger guy in the face with the back of the gun. The blow to the man's face caused the gun to fire. The lady thought I shot the man. She instantly laid face down on the floor and started crying for her life.

    The man I hit with the gun was dazed and bleeding profusely. He cupped his left eye with both hands to stop the bleeding. I didn't know who heard the shot so I started to panic. I yelled, "Turn the fuck around before I kill yall!" As they turned around with their backs facing me, I robbed them for everything they had. After I took their money and their remaining crack, I slowly backed towards the basement door. I yelled at them, "Better not fucking move!" and I ran out of the basement. Before I got to the alley, I could hear bullets ricocheting off of the building in front of me. I got low and I used a parked car to shield my body as I continued to run. I could hear police sirens approaching so I just kept running until the coast was clear. I know they could hear the sirens and would not follow me.

I went back home to count the money. It was less than $200 cash and several pieces of crack rock. I was pissed for a second but then thought, "It is more than I had." When I saw Justin's mom again I gave her a rock for the good Intel. We made that same kind of deal a few more times. She became so trustworthy that I paid her a rock before the robbery.

I eventually found out that her nephew was a big time drug dealer. I propositioned to give her three rocks to rob her nephew. She kept saying she didn't know if she wanted to do it. I gave my word that her nephew wouldn't be hurt. I also told her I would double her reward every deal after that. This robbery could be in the tens of thousands. I told Dee of the score because I would need help on this.

Dee and I were anxiously waiting on the details for this robbery. This could be the score that we dreamed of. I was broke, I needed this money. Finally Justin's mom agreed to help me set up her nephew. She was to find out exactly where he hung out so I could tail him. I was so eager to lock in our agreement that I gave her two rocks. Time went past and I didn't see her for a while.

I happened to be strolling on 119th street and ran into Justin's mom. When she saw me she made a fearful pause then continued towards me. She told me she had been looking for me to tell me she didn't want me to rob her nephew. I told her to give me my two rocks back. She said she didn't have them. Of course she didn't have them. She was a drug addict. I went on to tell her that by tomorrow, she needed to bring me an address or my two rocks, or I was going to kill her. All while this was happening Justin was reaching for me to pick him up.

Weeks went passed before I saw her again. When she saw me she started crying. I asked for what I wanted most, the address. She told me she didn't have it. I told her to give me the money for my two rocks. She cried saying she didn't have it. While she was cowering and crying, Justin was reaching for me to pick him up. As Justin leaned towards me, I grabbed him by the throat and snatch him out of her arms. I told her I would kill him if she didn't give me an address. She begged and pleaded for her son's life. She tried to snatch Justin from my grip so I grabbed her by the throat and threw her back. I yelled at her, "Give it up or he's gonna die!"

After over a minute of holding Justin by the throat, he turned blue and stopped breathing. I noticed he was dead so I dropped him to the ground. I walked over to choke her to death as well. I wasn't going to shoot her because a gun blast would have alerted possible witnesses or police. I couldn't let her live because I would have a witness against me for the murder of a toddler. As soon as my hand touched her throat, before I could squeeze, I heard a gasp from Justin. The baby's color was returning and he was gasping for air and crying loudly. I felt no need to protect myself, so as I walked away I told her, "You owe me for those two rocks. You stole from me!" I was hoping that those last words would compel her not to involve the cops. I never heard from or saw Justin or his mother again.

Stories of my brutal interaction with Justin and his mom spread all over. People really started fearing me. My name carried with it a sense of ruthlessness that few people had attained. Not only did I revel in the stories, I encouraged it. I wanted people to know what would happen if we had to clash. I was happy to know people were aware of the lengths I would go to settle a score. The more I hurt people, the less aware I was of my pain.

One day my father sent word though Dexter that he wanted to take us out to eat Chinese food. This was a shock! Was my father feeling guilty of something? To what do I owe this generosity? It didn't matter because I loved Chinese food, and I was not eating well. I fixed my attire in an attempt to mask the fact that I wasn't bathing regularly. It would have killed me for my father to find out that I was down on my luck.

I drove to the house and met with Tiffany, Dexter, and my father. Terrance would never do anything with my father. He hated my father more than I did. As we ate, my father never looked at me except to say hello. Tiffany was all giggles because we were together again. Halfway through the meal Dexter interrupted, "Daddy, did you know Luther almost killed a baby? He choked a baby and left it to die!" What the hell! How did he know this? Why in the fuck did he just repeat that? With extreme shock on his face my father asked if it was true. I looked my father in his eyes. I allowed him to stare into the depths of my hell bound soul. I smiled in an evil manner and replied in the affirmative as if it were nothing. On the inside I was hurt. My own brother just betrayed me…again. I began to daydream about all of the beatings that I took for Dexter. I was truly let down.

Life as a BD was pretty rough. There was very little of the glory that I believed was associated with it. Aside from gangbanging, I still played football. I continued to astonish other teams with my aggressive skills and ability to audible plays. I was the smallest guy on the field but my play always spoke the loudest. My gang life started being associated with me as well. Referees and recruiters warned me to straighten up before Universities viewed me as a liability. I scoffed at the notion, "Once a coach sees how I perform on the field, nothing else will matter." I couldn't have been more wrong. Recruitment letters stopped, except for some Division III schools. Recruiters didn't contact the coach at Simeon like they did when I played at Dunbar. I wondered if transferring to Simeon hindered me being recruited.

In an effort to unwind, another BD and I were going to his girlfriend's apartment. My car was down so we had to take the bus. His girlfriend invited a female friend over for me. When we arrived at her apartment and she buzzed us in. We walked up two flights of stairs. His girlfriend was in a robe waiting for us at the door. Her friend was waiting in the living room. We all walked to the living room and talked for a few minutes.

My fellow BD and his girlfriend departed to her bedroom. A few moments later you could hear them having sex. I looked at the girl sitting on the couch next to me and pulled her to me. I didn't know if she was going to accept my advances or push me away. I was too horny from the sexual sounds in the other room to care. I was pleased to feel no resistance as I pulled her into my chest. As I was kissing her, I slid off her clothes. I dominated her on that couch in many positions. I had a little bit more than she could handle. Every time she tried to run, I'd go even deeper to punish her. It seemed liked the rougher I got, the more sexual her moans became. She evidently liked it rough. Rough was my middle name so, I was happy to oblige.

About thirty minutes later, we left the house. As we were walking to the bus stop, we heard what we thought was glass breaking. We looked at the spot on the ground where we heard glass breaking. There was no broken glass anywhere. Less than a second later, a few feet from us, we heard the same sound again. This time we saw a chunk of concrete pop out of the spot where we heard the sound. The sound wasn't glass, but concrete being obliterated by a bullet. Somebody was sniper firing at us! There was a building behind us and no cars parked on that side of the street. We had no cover. We both got low. I told my fellow BD to run with me in the direction that I knew was away from the sniper's location. He panicked and took off in the opposite direction with no warning. I wasn't going to follow him because I knew it would put me into the direct line of fire. I ran to the bus stop and got on the bus. I went back to our set to tell what happened. We had a small set. Since nobody was hurt, they elected to leave it alone.

On a separate occasion I remember meeting a lady at a grocery store. She was about six feet tall and very curvaceous. Her silky hair stretched the length of her back. Her name was Tammie. Tammie lived right off of $63^{rd\ ST}$. You can tell she was very street smart. She asked if I was in a gang. I told her I was a BD. She was excited to hear that because she lived around all BD's. I exaggerated my financial status to impress her. I lied to her insinuating that I had a nice amount of drug money.

After talking dirty on the phone with Tammie for a few days, she finally agreed to let me come over for a sexual interlude. She asked me if I had any friends with money that I could introduce to her girlfriends. I told her I knew a few guys I could bring. I informed her I would bring three other guys with me. We arrived at her apartment around midnight on Saturday. As we were getting out of the car, I noticed Tammie was outside of the apartment. As soon as she saw me, she waved and told us to come up. Tammie went into the apartment without waiting on us.

Before I closed the driver's door, I noticed two men running from around Tammie's building towards us. The men made their move too soon. They should have waited until we got closer to the door, then they would have had us dead to rights. I yelled, "Look out!" I dropped to the floorboard to get my gun. The other guys were getting back into the car. I fired three shots in their direction to slow their approach. I didn't have enough bullets to shoot it out with them. We only had a few seconds, and then we all were dead! Guys were going to start pouring out of the buildings with guns.

After I fired three times, I jumped in the car; I put it in gear and started to pull off. I heard a banging on the rear passenger door. It was one of my guys. He did the right thing before he got out of my car and locked the door. Now he was locked out. The BD in front passenger side yelled, "They're gonna kill us, leave him!" The other guy in the backseat was bent over with his hands over his head. I yelled in panic, "Unlock the fucking door!"

The BD in the backseat temporarily snapped out of his state of panic. He reached over and unlocked the door. The door opened and the last BD jumped in. He dove into the car with his feet sticking out of the door. More and more gunshots started ringing out. As my windows were being shot out, I sped off. We stopped a few blocks down and checked for damage. Nobody was shot. Tammie set us up! As soon as we got to a payphone, we called Tammie's number. The first time I called she answered. When she discovered it was me, she just hung up. Every other time I called, a man picked up the phone. The man asked who I was and what I wanted with Tammie. I told him that she set us up and that we were going to kill her.

The man on the other line chuckled and told me to come back any time I wanted. I knew it was nothing I could do. I just had to let it go. The guys trying to rob us were definitely BD's. We were BD's from the 100's and they were from the low end. To them, we were not the same.

The guys who rode with me told how fearless I was during the set up. They mistook my ability to act in a crisis situation for lack of fear. They were wrong. I hated my life and I didn't care if I lived or died. It was my dream to go out in a blaze. I wanted to go out fighting. I had grandeur visions of taking out several adversaries on my last breath. I believed that was my only destiny. And I believed that I would meet my destiny before I turned eighteen. I knew one thing…no person on this earth would ever abuse me or cause me to cower.

I was getting into too many near death altercations. It seemed like every other day we were in a shootout. The weird thing is that I was more comfortable watching my back than things being calm. That fact might stem from the turmoil I grew up with while living at home.

I remember some of the BD's called me over to address where some men who were selling crack on our block. It was two of them. They weren't BD's and nobody knew them. They were older and way bigger than us. It was five of us. As we were walking in their direction, the two men noticed us. One man immediately ran. The other man yelled something at us and started shooting.

I remember having a rage that I have only had a few times in my life. While the bullets were flying, all of the BD's took cover. I didn't care about the bullets. I remember yelling, "You better kill me!" I then dashed across the street in his direction. I was about four strides into my sprint when I was tackled from behind. One of the BD's laid on top of me and yelled, "Stay down!" A few seconds later I noticed that there were no more gunshots. I violently pushed my fellow BD off of me. I hopped up and instinctively knew the man was out of bullets.

I ran straight towards the man who, just previously, was attempting to place bullets into my brain. It seemed like time stood still. I was filled with so much rage that I didn't have all my motor functions. I was so angry that my vision was distorted; kind of like I was in a haze. The next few moments seem to occur in slow motion. The shooter was obviously fearless and willing to engage in a fight. I didn't have the fluidness or the desire to move out of the way of his punches. I felt like a caveman on steroids. All my boxing skills were tossed out the window. I was going to take all the punishment he had, and see if he could handle mine. His first blow landed to my temple. I was rocked and immediately was dazed. He punched me again and more stars rang in my head. I threw a punch and it landed to his nose. The man stumbled back, while I continued with a barrage of thunderous blows. I hit him again and he started to go down. I jumped on top of his chest and continued to land powerful punches. After a few more punches, the man was conscious but concussed. He man laid flat on the concrete bleeding profusely and gurgling blood.

    The BD's pulled me off of the man reiterating the cops were coming. I broke lose only to unleash another endless flurry of punches. The guy who previously attempted to fill my body with bullets was unconscious and breathing erratically. I was filled with rage. My guys left me alone. They knew my anger would have allowed me to turn on them. The community never involves the police but rumors of me beating a much larger man to death spread like wildfire. Dexter told his friends that I beat a man to death. I remember his friend Nodisha questioned me about the beating. Every time there was a rumor that I killed someone, my brother was more than willing to help spread it. I knew Dexter was envious of me. But I never got used to the betrayal.

GUARDIAN ANGEL...RETIRED

I was in a very bad state. My hygiene was terrible due to an inability to bathe on a regular. My diet consisted of stolen cereal, corner store fast food, and Snickers bars. I robbed too many dealers where I hung out. The neighborhood was on high alert. The whole block seemed ready. They started shooting first and seeing who the person was later.

It was the middle of winter. I was a homeless seventeen year old on the Chicago streets. I was down to my last $20. I had nowhere to go to stay warm. I would never allow my father to know I was in a bad state. My pride wouldn't allow me. Dee was a fake friend, so I wasn't going to stay at his house. Then a thought popped into my head, "Find my mother, to see if she can help."

I looked up every Sandy or Sandra in the phone book. I didn't have enough money to call them all. I called all of the names that ended in Butler. That was a dead end. Those phone calls took my $20 down to $17. Now I tried the same thing with her maiden name. It was another dead end. I saw more names under the last name Davis. I didn't have enough money to call them all, but I was desperate. The first number was registered to a downtown address. I couldn't let the phone ring too many times. After the third ring, the call would go to the answering machine, and I would lose my money.

I dialed the first number. The phone rang once, and rang again. I had to hang up before the fourth ring. A lady picked up the phone on the third ring, "Davis residence, may I help you?" With a frog in my throat I asked, "I am looking for Sandra Ruth." The lady sternly asked, "Who's Calling?" I answered, "This is her son, Luther Butler." There was a brief pause and the lady replied, "Is that you Baby?" My heart started to palpitate. "Mom?" I inquired. "Oh my baby!" she exclaimed. I went on to tell her my predicament.

My mother told me that she lived with a man named Robert. Robert and my mother were on vacation in Las Vegas. She had her phone number forwarded. My mother told me that they would return Tuesday. It was the middle of winter in Chicago. Her return date was six days away, but my future seemed warm as a summer's day. I was elated. She gave me her cell phone number and her address. The next six days I did anything I could to stay warm; rode the transit bus from one end to another; stayed in the library all day, and use women for their apartments.

Tuesday finally came. I had butterflies for days prior. I didn't notice it but my nightmares of my mother were gone. I was still having nightmares of my father on a regular, but they had evolved. Sometimes in those nightmares I would barely overcome my father in combat. A lot of times it was a stalemate. Less often my father would stab me, but I awoke before he killed me. I went to a payphone to call my mother. I was waiting on a prerecorded message to say, "I'm sorry but the number you have reached has changed. No new information at this time!" Much to my surprise, my mother picked up on the second ring. She told me to bring just a few things and come right over.

My stomach was in knots. I jumped on the bus and headed to Randolph Street. I got off at Randolph Street and walked uphill three blocks to her apartment. Upon reaching the address, the first thing I noticed was a doorman. A freaking doorman! Are you kidding me? These weren't apartments at all, they were condominiums.

I saw expensive cars that I couldn't identify. I received disapproving looks from all of the uppity white people there. I proudly walked through the revolving doors and was immediately approached by a black doorman. He was about six feet tall, in his mid-50's with salt and pepper hair. The doorman asked, "Can I help you?" I replied, "Yes! I am here to see my mother Sandra Davis." He asked for a room number but through all of the excitement I forgot.

As I was being grilled, I noticed a listing of names and room numbers on a board in front of me. I pointed at the board and told the rude doorman the proper room number. He made no further attempts to assist me. After a few seconds of inaction, I attempted to access the elevator. The doorman immediately grabbed me by the shoulder. As soon as he touched me I whipped around and instinctively reached for the gun in the small of my back. The doorman retreated and yelled for the other doorman to call the police.

Through all of the commotion someone familiar with my mother or Robert must have notified her. My mother came downstairs and asked what was going on. I was still irrationally angry, but managed to tell her that I was grabbed why attempting to see her. She apologized to the doorman and notified him that I was her son. He reluctantly acquiesced and allowed me to board the elevator with my mother.

When I entered the condominium, I couldn't fight the slight feeling of disappointment. It was only a one bedroom. There wasn't a lot of room. She informed me that I could sleep on the couch, which converted into a bed. Then I saw a man come from the back room. He was dark skinned and about six feet tall. He had salt and pepper hair. His clothes smelled like Stetson cologne. He wasn't the most handsome man. He was really quiet. My mother introduced the man to me as her husband Robert. My mother told me that Robert has known me since I was born. She went on to tell me that Robert was a retired police officer of the Chicago Police Department. He was cop? How in the hell was I supposed to live there? I swallowed the frog in my throat and proceeded to greet him. I shook Robert's hand and said, "Hello Sir." Robert shook my hand and smiled. He seemed nice. His eyes read no judgment. His body language screamed, "Fuck with me if you want to!"

Over the next few days Robert barely spoke a word to me. I knew he was scrutinizing my every move. That Thursday my mom had to make a run. As we were sitting, Robert questioned me. He asked me which gang I was in. He asked me why I banged. He asked me what I wanted out of life. I knew I couldn't lie to Robert, so I told him the truth. He never judged me once. He warned me of the dangers of gang life. Robert also admonished that if I lived there, I would have to give that life up.

Robert told me I was a good kid born in a bad situation. He told me that my mother and father both have their problems, but I owed it to myself to rise above it. He laid down the rules of the house and told me that he was glad I was there. He stood up, gave me a brief smile and headed back to his room. Before he entered his room, he stopped and said, "I know you have a gun. Place all your guns in that black bag under the table tonight. Once you turn twenty-one, I will give them back to you." I didn't even know this man, but I felt more comfortable and secure with him than anybody had made me feel in my entire life. Before he fully entered his room I replied, "I don't want it back!"

I was praying he read through my statement and disposed of the gun. If ballistics were performed, I would probably get the death penalty. Robert popped his head from out of his room. I was prepared for him to tell me to leave his apartment after my last remark. Instead Robert remarked, "How are you gonna get foxes with those threads? We're going to go clothes shopping this weekend."

The weekend came and Robert woke me up to go clothes shopping. We went to several department stores. Out of respect, I chose the cheapest items. He would throw the parsimonious garbs back and exclaim, "Get what you want!" Robert bought me several pairs of Nike's, about ten jogging suit sets, shirts, pants, socks, and underwear.

Every store we entered, my mother would tell Robert to stop buying me stuff. She fussed that he was spending too much money on me. My mother surprised me with her jealousy. Robert surprised me with his unlimited generosity. When we arrived back at the condominium, I was elated. My mother was upset. She left, making sure she slammed the door on the way out.

As we were sitting alone, I turned to Robert to thank him. As I opened my mouth, a rush of emotion came over me. I attempted to tell him that I appreciated all that he had done for me. I wanted to tell him that nobody has ever shown this kind of generosity to me. As soon as I attempted to open my mouth I noticed tears pooling in the wells of my eyes. Out of embarrassment, I walked to the bathroom to get a hold of my emotions and wipe my tears away. I looked in the mirror at my overly emotional ass. I glared at my tear filled reflection to harden up. After spending a few minutes in the bathroom, I exited.

With a steady resolve, I walked right to Robert and thanked him for all of his generosity. He then went into his pocket and pulled out $100. Robert then stated, "Here is some money. You don't have to worry about getting clothes or money, so that only leaves you to focus on school. There is a car in the garage for you to drive back and forth to school. It's not for you to drive around with your friends. It is for you to get to school and date some foxes. You need to start pulling away from your gang ties because you will have a future." He then placed his hand on the back of my head like a father would do his son. The emotional floodgates were ready to run. I was trying to hold back. I was one of the toughest kids I know. I can't be crying! I dropped my head to hide my emotions and sobbingly whispered, "Thank You!" Robert knew I was an emotional wreck. He then went into his room, which allowed me time to straighten up.

My mother and I never bonded. She wasn't like I remembered her. I inquired about the rest of her family. I asked her the whereabouts of my sister Jen. She didn't know. I asked her how Foxy was doing. She said fine, but she wouldn't call Foxy. I later found out that she has stolen some things from Foxy and was avoiding her. My mother made a phone call and handed me the phone. While the phone was ringing, I asked my mother, "Who is this?" My mother replied, "It's your great grandmother." When my great grandmother answered the phone, she asked me why I called her. Before I could answer, my great grandmother notified me to never contact her again. She allowed the continuous rape of my sister, Jen. I never wanted to talk to her anyway.

Everybody in school noticed my instantaneous metamorphosis. The rumors floated about me selling drugs. I didn't do much to dispel the rumors. While attempting to withdraw from gang life, I noticed the gang life for what it was. It was a negative plight that stained the inner city.

I had friends in every gang. Every so often, one of those friends would call me about my little brother, Dexter. They would tell me that they had my brother Dexter and that I should come and get him before they kill him. It seemed as if my brother was faking gang affiliations and started banging like he was a BD. Sometimes he would threaten if someone touched him that I would kill them. Dexter never seemed to grasp that I was one of many terrors in Chicago. There were thousands of killers in Chicago, who could give a rat's ass what I was capable of.

My brother was so envious of me, but he constantly used my name in times of trouble. We were not close but I loved him. I tried to keep him safe. I even took Dexter and informed our father of what was going on. My father never addressed my brother. Instead, my father seemed more irritated at how nice I was dressed and the fact that I drove a nice car. I sprung at the chance to throw Robert's generosity in my father's face. My father interrupted me by saying, "Robert must be retarded to help you! Why would he help a gangbanger?"

I calmly told my father that Robert wanted me to focus on getting into college. My father laughed and replied, "What are you gonna do to get into college? Nobody is recruiting you anymore. I haven't seen a recruitment letter in months! I never thought you were that good anyway. I would have run circles around you if I were your age!" With a respectful resolve I replied, "You never played defense, so how do you know? And what type of father discourages his kids from being the best that they can be? What type of man beats his women and kids bloody?"

My father knew not to get aggressive. I would have probably let emotions overcome me and beat him to death. My father turned to my brother and asked, "Did I ever beat you or your mother?" Dexter immediately replied, "No Sir." Dexter kept his eyes on his father the entire time. He never looked at me once. I knew why my brother did it. A boxer gets hit in his face thousands of times, but the blow hurts just the same. I felt the same way about Dexter's betrayal.

I tried hard to pull myself from the gang life. It was way harder than I thought. It was a gang war in Chicago. A lot of those wars were fought in the schools. I ended up being suspended from Simeon for a few gang fights. I decided to start hanging out with my old friend and teammate from Dunbar High School. I called Poodle and he was ecstatic to hang out. Things went well for a while, but Poodle's insecurities started to arise again. He pulled me to the side and told me not to be friendly with any of his children's mothers. I told him that I loved him and I would never betray our friendship. I told him that I was unable to be curt with the mother of his children. I was nothing like his other friend who had sex with his ex. If anything, I considered his ladies as my sisters and would look after them as such.

I thought the issue was resolved. One night we went to a solon to pick up Danielle, one of the mothers of his children. They sat in the front seats of the car and I was in the back. Danielle turned towards the backseat and asked me how I was doing. I told her fine. Poodle instantly yelled, "Dammit Luther! Stop talking to her!" Danielle scoffed at his attempted chastisement and continued to speak to me. I replied, "There are three people in this car, she can't just speak to you!"

Poodle slammed on the brakes of his 1996 mustang and yelled, "Get out of my car!" Danielle tried to reason with him, but it was evident that now she was intimidated by his actions. I exclaimed, "You want me to get out here? This is Black Stone territory. I can't get out here. They will light my ass up!" Poodle said, "Well you should have listened when I told you not to talk to Danielle!"

I got out and started walking towards the bus stop. As I was walking, five men approached me from behind. I could tell they were following me. I slowed down to show that I was not scared of them. Slowing down also shortened the distance between us. If they had guns, I would be better able to defend myself in close proximity.

The men started asking me where I was from. I never answered. One of the guys yelled, "That's a bad ass leather coat…take it off!" If this isn't karma, then I don't know what is. Am I about to get robbed for the same leather jacket I robbed someone else for? Before I knew it one of the guys attempted to snatch the jacket off of me. The jacket ended up going over my head. I felt what seemed like an endless number of blows. Several times I was dazed. Fearful that I was about to be shot, I quickly slipped out of the jacket and threw up my guards. The guys surrounded me.

I was in full fight mode now. All my senses were in tuned. I hit one guy in the face and he fell back. Another one of the guys threw a haymaker. I slipped that punch like a professional boxer and punched the guy closest to me. I landed a perfect punch to his nose. The guy fell and balled up. The guys reformed their semi-circle around me. They kept yelling for one another to rush me but they were too scared to receive one of my Mike Tyson like blows.

After a few seconds of bouncing around, they ran away. I knew when they returned, that I was dead. I picked up my jacket and continued to walk to the bus stop. Running would have caused too much attention in that neighborhood. I safely made it to the bus stop. As I was standing at the bus stop, an older Mercedes Benz passed me. The driver slowed down when the car was in front of me. I couldn't see the driver. The driver of the Benz circled around the block to see my face again. I knew gun shots were about to ring out. I wanted to run but there was nowhere to go. The Benz made a U-turn and was heading back in my direction.

As the Benz was in front of me, I noticed a dark colored box Chevrolet in the street to my right. The driver of the Chevrolet drove slowly and was block from me. The driver turned off the lights of the Chevrolet and continued to drive towards me. Shit! I knew a drive-by was imminent now! I tightened up my body to prepare for the bullets. The Benz sped past me towards the Chevrolet. The driver of the Benz stepped out of the car and talked to the driver in the Chevrolet.

The Benz put the car in reverse and stopped right in front of me. The driver leaned over and opened the passenger door. I heard a voice yell, "Get in!" I looked inside to see a man named Shareef. Shareef worked at Simeon High School. I exclaimed, "Shareef! I am so glad to see you!" He asked, "What are you doing in my neighborhood? Those dudes were about to kill you!"

Shareef dropped me off at a female acquaintance's house. I had to clean up. I had a bloody mouth, blood running out of my left ear canal, and a bloody shirt. I was still in shock with how Poodle kicked me out of his car. That was the first in a series of events that ended our relationship. Life shouldn't be this hard.

    Living with Robert was excellent. He was gentle, caring, intelligent, and genuinely concerned for my well-being. We did things like father and son. We went for long rides and talked about life. Robert taught me how to play checkers. We would play for hours. I never even came close to beating him. He loved the Chicago Bulls, so we would sit and watch every game. He showed me how to properly shoot a gun. He preached on a daily about me becoming a positive role model. Robert represented everything that is good in man. I loved him more than anyone on earth.

    I had no real interaction with my mother. The only time I went somewhere with her was when I drove her to the projects so she could purchase crack. I would take her every two or three days. I detested the fact that she was not the best woman for Robert. Robert frequently found her incoherent in the condominium hallway. She was always high. I never asked Robert why he was with her because I already knew. My mother was pretty. She erased all animosity Robert had with her actions by incorporating a superfluous sex life. Robert wasn't the most attractive man. I believe he traded a lot for a pretty woman who made him feel like a king.

    My mother never hid her unhappiness with Robert taking care of me financially. She always said Robert spent money on me that she could have enjoyed. My mother forced me to pay her a percentage of the allowance that Robert gave me. She said if I told Robert, she would in turn force him to put me out. I paid her 1/3 of the allowance Robert gave to me. But that still wasn't enough. My mother started cutting up my clothes. I had to keep my clothes with a girlfriend of mine. I didn't like my mother so I knew I had to graduate from high school and leave.

    My problems at home were compounded by my problems in the street. I regrettably recall a day when one of the BD's was murdered. He attended Simeon with us. His nickname was MaiTai. He was a person that everyone liked. He was murdered for refusing to halt his drug sales on a particular block. Rivals from another gang made light of his death by making some derogatory remarks about MaiTai. I got the call to retaliate for those remarks. I was livid. I would have killed these guys' whole family if I had the chance. I raced to Robert's condominium to get my all black gloves, black hat, black pants, black shirt, and black shoes.

While I was hastily ruffling though my clothes, Robert entered the condominium. He asked what I was doing. I tried to brush him off, but he was on to me. I had packed all my black gear in a bag and was about to leave. Robert raised his finger and said, "Wait one minute." I had to go! What does he want? Robert came out with his 38 revolver in his hand and said, "Alright…let's go."

Shocked, I asked, "What are you doing?" Robert replied, "I love you. I told you I was gonna get you through high school. I would never let anyone hurt you…not even yourself. I know I can't stop you. So, if you're going to do something wrong, I am going with you!" I dropped the bag and started crying uncontrollably. As I was crying, Robert hugged me. He offered gentle words to console me. I was so depressed. Why couldn't he have been my real father? I would have been a straight A student. I could have become someone great. Robert would never have helped in a shootout. He was using love to conquer evil…and it worked. That was my last day as a Black Disciple.

One day I received a phone call from my father. He asked me to talk to Dexter. He said Dexter was trying to go down the wrong path. My father said some of his students informed him that Dexter was still falsely claiming to be a BD. I was a little confused. My father and I had no relationship, so why would he call upon me for a favor? The last time I checked, Dexter was running around with two bisexual boys calling himself Alize'! I believed my brother was sexually confused. Dexter had a few androgynous traits. My father sought to eliminate many of those traits by constantly accusing my brother of being a sissy, punk or faggot. If he was gay or bisexual, my father made it impossible for Dexter to be comfortable with that lifestyle.

I had a strong inclination that at the very least, Dexter was bisexual. One instance occurred when I was visiting my brother at my father's house. I walked upstairs to find my brother and his friend using their hands to muffle their giggles, while they huddled to listen to whoever was on the other end of the phone. I asked my brother what they were doing. He muted the phone and handed the receiver to me. While on the phone I heard what I believed to be a male having sexual relations. I pulled my ear from the phone and asked, "What is that?" Dexter laughingly informed me that he and his other male friend convinced the male on the phone to masturbate while they listened. I frustratingly inquired, "Why would you do that? What is so funny about that? Why would you be amused at hearing a guy jerk off?" Dexter became upset with me and replied, "Whatever!"

I couldn't focus on Dexter. I was busy trying to graduate. I had to go to college. I had to get away from my drug addict of a mother. I was tired of her robbing me blind. Senior year was a little bit of a struggle. My pride allowed me to slip. I got suspended a few times for fighting. I ditched school a lot. I saw school as a required burden, not as a tool to enhance my socioeconomic standing.

My high school football career ended with a bang. I played excellent the entire year, but I still wasn't being recruited. All the schools that had been recruiting me wanted nothing to do with an unstable gangbanger. In May of 1994, I graduated from Simeon Vocational High School. I invited Dexter, Fran, Tiffany, Terrance, and Robert to my graduation. Inviting Robert meant inviting my mother. Dexter didn't show up. I am not sure if my father had anything to do with that. At the graduation, my mother was embarrassingly under the influence of narcotics. Robert was poised as ever. Fran was happy to see me graduate. Graduating was bittersweet to me. I had done too much damage to myself to feel secure in my future.

Graduating from high school left me with the realization that college was out of the question. Robert coaxed me into joining the Air Force. My test scores were good enough to get me a higher rank. I went to MEPS, got sworn into the Air Force, and had my date set for boot camp. In the weeks to follow, I had to stay away from my mother, so I hung with the BD's again. I was drinking heavily day and night. I had one last drinking binge before I was to ship out. It was about 3am and I was on my way to Robert's condominium.

In a drunken stupor, I fell asleep at the wheel. I ran a red light and hit an off duty policeman. The first impact concussed me so bad that my speech was incoherent gibberish. My car spun violently and wrapped around a pole. The second impact of hitting the pole snapped out of my concussed state. Before my car hit the pole, I ran over a pedestrian.

When I became coherent, I noticed deep gashes on my head and a chipped tooth. The width of the car was reduced to less than half. The front passenger door was pushed all the way to my right arm. I was lucky to be alive. I climbed through the window only to see a white male lying on his back. The man had been gutted from his privates to his sternum. I could see his insides! He reached his hand out to me and exclaimed, "I am dying man!" In a daze, I looked over at the vehicle I hit. A black off duty police officer walked out of the car unharmed. I was cited for falling asleep at the wheel and running a red light.

I refused medical treatment and walked over a mile to Robert's condominium. I woke my mother while entering the apartment. My mother asked why I was so bloody and I told her the story. My mother exclaimed, "Robert! Robert, get in here! Luther has put us in the poor house! Oh my God we are going to lose everything!" Robert calmly entered the living room. I told him what happened. He reassured me everything was going be ok. He gave me a hug and they retreated to their bedroom.

I don't remember if the man I hit lived or died. I was too scared to ask Robert. I do remember Robert receiving a civil lawsuit in regards to the accident. The fact that I caused Robert to get sued was too much for me to bear. The Air Force recruiter informed me to schedule another boot camp date after I handled my court hearings stemming from the accident. My mother now made it unbearable to live with. She hated me for the financial obligation I now placed on Robert. I started staying more over Dee's house. I didn't like him much. But misery loves company…and boy were we a miserable pair.

R.I.P. LIL YUMMY

It was the fall of 1994. The BD's got into a shootout. I remember Lil Yummy was all over the news. In the midst of the shootout, he ended up shooting and killing a young girl. Lil Yummy was on the run. There was a big manhunt for an eleven year old killer. After a couple of days on the run, Lil Yummy was found dead! He had a single gunshot to the back of the head. The kid was murdered execution style on his knees.

They found tear trails on Yummy's face. Before he was murdered he was probably crying and begging for leniency. I was informed that same day that Yummy's murder was ordered by the BD's. The BD's feared because of Lil Yummy's age, he would succumb to police interrogation. He knew the inner circle and was privy to many murders. To the BD's, he was a liability. To me, he was a kid whom we led straight to his untimely death.

Before a shootout, the BD Minister would yell, "Think like a killer!" I thought killers were supposed to stick together. How could we raise this preteen to be a killer and kill him for doing the exact thing we raised him to do? I was upset that I wasn't with Lil Yummy. I would have shot till my last bullet then fought till my last breath to protect him. I failed Yummy. I was a part of this little kid's murder. Every time I interfered with his grandparents getting Lil Yummy, I murdered him. I put the bullet in the back of Yummy's head, every time I ignored the opportunity to steer him in the right direction. A few weeks later, Lil Yummy was featured on the cover Life Magazine. Tupac even made mention of Yummy in one of his songs. His murder hit me hard. I was left battling my depression. With all my strengths and leadership qualities, I choose to lead people down the wrong path.

UNIVERSITY WOES

A booster for Morris Brown College in Atlanta contacted my father. He told my father that Morris Brown could use me. They didn't offer any scholarships because they were a smaller school. They promised me that financial aid would take care of all college costs. To play for such a small college was an insult to my athletic ability. But beggars can't be choosers.

Robert bought me a plane ticket to Atlanta. He offered to give me money, but I refused. The guilt of me causing a civil suit against him was too much for me to bear. Morris Brown seemed to be in a state of destitution. The football team had no weight room. There were a few free weights scattered at the end of a hallway in the dorms. Their football equipment was run down. My high school team was better than this team. Their most talented athlete was a receiver from Chicago.

My attempts to register for school resulted in utter confusion. There was no record of me, even though I registered before I arrived. Atlanta was not only humid, but it was Africa hot! During summer camp it was evident that I would not receive a fair shake. The coaches pushed for their southern boys to play.

Time there was frustrating. I began to bond with one of the guys on the team. We called him "C". "C" was a street boy from Ohio. He reminded me of my guys from back home. I started falling into my old ways. I bought a new 9mm pistol from a guy pedaling guns at the school.

One day I entered my teammate's room to see all of the guys staring out of the window. They were watching the local thugs steal the subwoofers out of one of the teammate's van. I yelled, "Let's go fuck them up!" They said it was too many of them. I pointed to the guy whose van was being vandalized and replied, "You have a gun, shoot them!" He sarcastically replied, "You shoot them." I stuck out my hand to receive his gun. I took the semi-automatic pistol and aimed it at the vandals. They were approximately 200 yards away in the parking lot. One of my teammates screamed, "No!" and pushed my hands down. Another one of the teammates called the police. I later found out that the team had been clashing with the local thugs for a while.

One day during summer camp, "C" and I were hanging around in my room. We were resting from early morning practice. We were disturbed by our other teammates banging on my door. They said the hoods from Atlanta were outside Morris Brown picking a fight with several teammates. I ran outside with my gun tucked in the back of my pants. I witnessed several big men threatening some of my teammates. As I approached, the local boys surrounded me. "C" covered my backside in an attempt to keep me from being attacked from behind. There were at least twenty adversaries from Atlanta. All of them were country big. As they surrounded the two of us, I pulled out the gun from the small of my back. As soon as I pulled out the gun, the women started screaming, "Don't shoot them Chi-Town...please don't shoot them!" The pandemonium spread fear in the guys from Atlanta and caused them to hastily retreat.

Atlanta police arrived on the scene, so I ran back to my room to hide the gun. The next day I was summoned in the Dean's office to answer charges of brandishing a firearm. I lied and claimed that I never had a gun. The Dean informed me that several witnesses gave the same details, all the way down to the description of the gun. The Dean notified me that I was being watched.

A few days later, some of the teammates entered my room with bloody lips. They informed me that the same guys from Atlanta attacked them. I grabbed my gun and we went on the hunt for the assailants. While driving down a busy street, one of the teammates yelled, "Those are the guys who jumped on us!" It was five men walking down the street. I yelled, "Stop the car!" "C" and I jumped out and fought all five of the boys. We beat the guys up pretty bad. Two guys ended up on the ground unconscious and the other three ran away. I took the wallets, watches, and jewelry of the unconscious men. We jumped back into the van and went back to Morris Brown College.

Hours later the police placed the whole football team in a lineup. "C" and I were picked out of the lineup and charged with aggravated battery and robbery. It took me weeks to get word to Robert that I was jailed. He finally ended up getting me a bail bondsman and I was released. I returned to Morris Brown only to find out that I was kicked out. I wasn't upset that I was being charged. I could care less that I was kicked out of college. It saddened me to know that I let Robert down. He viewed me in a more positive light than I viewed myself.

What made matters even worse; the men we beat up weren't involved in fight with my teammates. One of the guys I robbed was studying to be a preacher. He refused to testify against us. The charges against me ended up being dropped. The flight back to Chicago was dreadful.

My mother made a point to let me know that I was impeding on her lifestyle. She made it known that she didn't want me living with her anymore. I was tired of her extorting money from me and vandalizing my possessions. I visited Robert almost every day but I rested my head usually over Dee's house.

The same family friend that referred me to Morris Brown referred me to a junior college in Albuquerque, New Mexico. The junior college had a struggling football team and was in need of some talent. The college was New Mexico Military Institute. This was an officer candidacy school. Robert believed military structure could help me to become a man. If I graduated from there, I would be an officer in the Army. I decided to go.

I struggled with the new military lifestyle. New recruits were treated like the scum of the earth. This was a hard adjustment for me because I always equated military with might. With that being the case, I should already have rank because I could physically take on these guys ten at a time. I dominated the physical training. New recruits and officers alike were in awe at how fast I could complete a training course.

Practicing with the football team was too easy. I dominated without even trying. I became the starting free safety and running back. My immaturity prevented me from progressing to the militaristic lifestyle. It was hard for me to take orders from a person that had the physical stature of Lindsay Lohan. In Chicago, I was in battles. I was war tested. They only study battle theories. That mindset halted my ability to advance there.

You weren't allowed to have sexual relations there. The men outnumbered the women six to one. My inner desires were getting the best of me. I met a black lady who had a French name. Her name was Monplaisur. Her name literally translated to "My Pleasure". Monplaisur had smooth caramel skin. She was nicely built with a short hairstyle. She was hyper sexual so I used her to fulfill my needs. One day Monplaisur decided to confide in me. She informed me that she was molested by her father her entire life. It was sick irony that the man who illegally satisfied his sexual urges with his daughter, named her "My Pleasure". She noticed how I carried myself and asked if I could help her. "What do you want me to do?" I inquired. She immediately replied, "You can kill him!"

I laughed it off. For about a month Monplaisur continued to tell me of different accounts of her father's molestation. When Christmas break was near, Monplaisur blurted out, "The semester's almost up! I'm going to have to go back home to my father! He's going to rape me again! I will pay you to kill him!" The only part of her statement I heard was "I'll pay you." I interrupted her mid plea and asked, "How much?" She asked, "How much does it cost to have someone killed?" I exclaimed, "How the hell am I supposed to know!"

I told Monplaisur it would cost $5,000! I was hoping this amount was too much money and she would just give up on the whole idea. She agreed. I was taken back. I was looking for an out. I was expecting her to say she didn't have it. Her next question was, "When can you do it?" I replied, "Whoa! I'm not doing shit until I have $1,000 down!" She said she didn't have that much. "My Pleasure" gave me around $600 before we went on break. Upon handing me the money she said, "You have to kill my father while we are on break. I will give you my address and phone number." I immediately took the money to a tattoo shop. I got a tattoo on the right side of my back in memory of my murdered sister Cheryl.

Right before Christmas break, I was called into the school's office. I was informed that I would not be welcomed back to the school after the semester ended. They informed me that I had been cited for being too aggressive, combative, and insubordinate. This was good news because I didn't want to be there anymore. I definitely wasn't going to kill Monplaisur's father. I knew would never see her again. I immediately thought of Robert. How can I let him down again? What the fuck was wrong with me? Why can't I just be a people person? Robert flew my sorry ass back to Chicago yet again.

I felt so low. It seemed that I was destined to let my mentor and my father figure down. Then I had an idea; contact some of the schools that had been recruiting me as a junior. I sent my highlight film to about ten schools. The first one to contact me was the Northwestern University's defensive back coach. He wanted to meet me in person. Yes! This is the break I was waiting on. In the meeting he told me that he knew who I was and that I was an excellent player. He went on to tell me that he didn't need any more defensive backs. He said since I was fast, that I would be a nice back up to their starting running back and Heisman Trophy candidate, Darnell Autry.

What the hell! I am nobody's backup! I haven't played a down for them but he already had me boxed in a certain supporting role. To add insult to injury, he informed me that they could only offer a partial scholarship. I was financially unable to take care of the remaining balance.

The next college to contact me was Illinois State University. The defensive back coach's name was Coach Byas. He showed a lot of interest in me. He wanted me to play there. He told me that I would have to earn a scholarship and a starting spot. Since no other colleges really wanted to have anything to do with me, I went to Illinois State. I had a whole semester to prepare before I enrolled at Illinois State. I decided to take care of some core classes at Olive Harvey Community College.

I raced to tell Robert the good news. Robert wasn't as elated as I expected him to be. He looked me into my eyes and said, "I am not going to be around forever. I need to know that you are going to make it!" With conviction I told Robert that I was changing my ways.

Enrolling at Olive Harvey College was a good introduction to college life. I started to develop a sense of self pride. Most of the classes were easy. The professors were eager to help a football star, who had fallen from glory, back to his feet. Those teachers were my inspiration.

While attending Olive Harvey, I met a girl named Mimi. Mimi was a pretty, light skinned girl with long hair. She dressed nice and had a nice frame to go with it. She was a little ghetto, so that fit well with me. Mimi and I started dating. She knew all about my abusive past. I didn't talk to her much about my street life. I didn't talk a whole lot to her…she did more than enough talking for the both of us. I introduced her to my mother and Robert. Robert really liked her. I don't think my mother was ever sober enough to realize that I was introducing her to my girlfriend. I was bouncing back and forth between Dee's home, Robert's place, and even my father's place. I warned her of my father so she was prepared. She always spoke to my father. She was very respectful. She even cooked meals for him.

I learned something about myself while dating Mimi. I learned that I needed a woman around. I learned that I needed a woman to sleep by me. It helped to ease the frequency of the nightmares of my mother and my father. Mimi was my second girlfriend. The idea of having a girlfriend was so erotic. I was in the newlywed stage with her. Our interaction was passionate, taboo, and exciting. I spent every waking moment with her. She was my escape to life. She was already in love. I was so jaded by life that at the time I was incapable of loving her. Hell…I didn't even love myself! Even though I didn't love her, I needed her. I did, however, love how Mimi made me feel.

I was a month away from going to Illinois State. I recall one evening when my father called me downstairs. When I got downstairs my father said, "I don't want Mimi to come over my house anymore!" My heart started jumping out of my shirt. I yelled, "Why?" He replied, "I don't trust her…she doesn't have long conversations with me!" I lashed back, "She is my girlfriend, not yours! She has no reason to have long conversations with you!"

I rebutted, "She has cooked multiple dinners for you! She says hello every time she sees you. She has never been disrespectful to you ever!" He replied, "Well after today, she is no longer allowed IN MY HOUSE!" Fran was visiting my father from one of her many hiatuses. She heard the commotion and came into the living room. As soon as Fran entered the living room, my father blurted out, "You think you are so mature. You're not even that good of a football player. I would have wiped you under the table!" I replied, "Those are words of envy. I am smarter, faster, and stronger than you ever were. Oh! And by the way, I looked you up on the Chicago Bears roster. I know you never played a down for them. You lied to everybody about the one touchdown you scored for the Bears. One day I will play pro football and I will get a touchdown with my hands tied behind my back!" My father replied, "If that is how you feel, then you are no longer welcome here either!" I only stayed there a few nights while visiting my brother. His actions didn't bother me much. I would be in college soon, and my sweetheart Mimi would be joining me there as well.

Weeks passed and I was at summer camp at Illinois State University. It is about 170 degrees outside but I was elated to have a chance to showcase my talent. I was fourth stream on the depth chart. It didn't bother me because I knew it would change before long. Only 1st through 3rd stream got rotations during practice. My job was to hand out water with the water boy. Days of this passed. Then weeks of this passed. I was starting to lose hope. Finally one day the coach called me in. I was ready. I knew my position like the back of my hand. The quarterback hikes the ball. It is a running play to the opposite side of the field. The coach pulled me out after that play. I exclaimed, "Let me show you what I can do coach!" Coach Byas said, "Don't worry you'll get your chance." I was brimming with emotional doubt. There was no way for me to level the playing field. Screw college! Life if just not fair!

The starting cornerback was injured so I was moved up to 3rd stream. A man, who was rumored to be a pro scout, attended our practice session. He was there to see the starter but the starter was hurt. The scout decided to stay anyway. I was ready to shine. It was almost the end of practice and the coach still hadn't put me into the rotation. With only a few minutes left in practice Coach Byas put me in. The quarterback snapped the ball. It was a pass play. I read the receiver and shadowed him. The ball was passed to my man. As soon as the ball touched his hands, I landed one of the most bone crushing tackles that I have ever delivered.

The receiver dropped the ball and withered on the ground in pain. My teammates and coaches all exclaimed at once, "OHHHHHHH!" I overheard Coach Byas tell the head coach, "That had to be a fluke!" After the trainers carted the injured receiver off of the field, practice resumed. The center snaps the ball again. It was a run play to my side. I made the tackle in the backfield. The hit left a resounding bass sound as I made impact with the running back. The defensive players are all celebrating over my hit.

The head coach yells out, "Ok, last play…let's make it count!" We all readied for the final play of practice. The center hikes the ball. It's another pass play! The receiver I am defending runs full speed towards me, then quickly turns to face the quarterback. The quarterback quickly throws the football to my receiver. The receiver catches the ball. Before he takes one step, I tackle him from behind. The hit sounded like a shotgun being fired. The receiver lay on the ground yelling in pain.

I wasn't pumped but rather offended that it took so long for the coaches to give me a shot. With aggressive rage I yelled, "This is my field! Nobody out here can do what I do!" I heard the recruiter tell Coach Byas, "You've got something there!"

The head coach walked over to me. I was gloating. I was waiting for him to kiss my ass too. The head coach said, "I am from down south. It is different than Chicago. My players make good tackles and help the receivers back up."
ME: "I was not taught to play like that. I knock them down to keep them down. They will be afraid to catch the ball when I am around."
Head Coach: "Well…in my system you will help the receivers up after you tackle them!"
Me: "I can't do that!"

Head Coach: "Well you will never start for me!"
Me: "Who is going to outplay me?"

One of my teammates budded in, "You shouldn't talk to the coach like that." The coach politely walked away. I continued to dominate in practice. I could not wait for the season to start. A month before the season opener, the head coach called me into his office. He told me no matter how good I was that I would never start for him. He told me that I was too aggressive. He told me that I made my teammates more aggressive. He said I was out of control and a liability. I was stuck in the victim mentality. I was not mature enough to understand the concerns my coach had for me.

My self-worth was determined by how I protected my friends. I protected the people I cared for my whole life. I was feeling down because of football. I was missing the intimate interaction with Mimi. I couldn't wait for her to enroll at Illinois State. In the meantime there were beautiful women of all races throwing themselves at the football players. I was not used to it.

My immaturity allowed me to abuse the position. Since Mimi's not here, I might as well indulge a little. One thing I would not compromise was my sexual safety. I always used a condom. One summer night a pretty, light complexioned woman visited me in my apartment. She had a boyfriend, but said I really turned her on. She was very aggressive. She walked right to my bedroom and sat on my bed. As soon as I crossed the threshold into my bedroom, this lady was all over me. As we kissed, the redbone undressed both of us. The night was steamy. She liked rough necks and I was as rough as they came. In the moment of our 'rough conversation' the condom broke. We stopped and got another condom. I was never alarmed because she was so clean you could eat off of any part of her body.

The next weekend Mimi drove down to visit me. Her visit was spurred by her horniness more than anything else. Mimi left back to Chicago a few days later. After a week of normal conversation, Mimi called me cursing. Mimi said she returned from her gynecologist and that she had gonorrhea! She asked me who I cheated on her with. I denied having sex with any other woman. I fed her a quick excuse to get off the phone. I had to think. I knew I always wore a condom. Then I remembered. The condom did break with that one girl…crap! But she was so clean. I called the condom breaker on the phone and she sadly replied, "Oh no! My boyfriend gave it to me. I didn't think I gave anything to you." I hung up the phone, dreading having to call Mimi back.

    My ghetto ass girlfriend is going to stab me! I might not have been in love with Mimi but I never wanted to bring any harm to her. I cared for her. With my tail tucked, I called Mimi back and confessed everything. My sexual indiscretion had a twofold effect on my relationship. It caused Mimi to become aggressive with me, and it caused me to react more aggressively to control her. I started grabbing and snatching Mimi around. I was ignorant to the fact that even though I was not striking her, I was being abusive to my significant other; just like my father.

JAIL BIRD

    Classes were in session. College was going fine. Mimi and I were doing well. It was a few weeks from our season opener. It was a Friday afternoon. One of my teammates got into a fight with a man over a basketball game. The man retreated with threats of bringing his family from St. Louis to shoot my teammate. The whole team dismissed the threat. Around ten p.m. that night, I received a frantic knock on my dorm door. Fearful, players told me that the man brought his family from St. Louis. To make matters worse, one of the men brandished a gun.
    I put on my clothes and headed downstairs. It was evident that the campus police were too scared to disperse the armed St. Louis clan. I listened to the clan hurl numerous death threats at my teammates. I just lost it! I ran past the police and threw a haymaker at the gun toting thug. The blow caused both of us to fall, with me being on top of him. My victim was underneath me mumbling incoherently. The campus police pepper sprayed the man underneath me and placed me into handcuffs.

The guys from St. Louis hastily dispersed to avoid arrest. I was the only idiot arrested. The fight made the local media. I was being charged with a felony aggravated battery. I called Robert and he bailed me out of jail. He retained a lawyer for me and drove home without telling my mother.

Immediately after bonding out of jail, I became the school hero. The jubilee from my heroism was overshadowed by a statement released to the press from my head coach. The statement declared the incident was not a reflection of the football program because I had been ineligible to play. The head coach just lied!

The head coach called me to his office the next Monday. He informed me that I was no longer on the team. I was crushed. I tried to explain that I was sticking up for a teammate. My pleas landed on deaf ears. I didn't know how to handle my spontaneous rages. I continued to put others above my well-being. Depression started settling in. How do I explain this one to Robert? How could I let him down again? Am I destined to lose, or am I just a loser? I couldn't eat for a few days. I received financial aid and took out student loans to pay for college.

I had to find a way to provide the necessities. I landed a job at APAC telemarketing firm as a telemarketer. I gave in and finally decided to call Robert and tell him the bad news. It deeply saddened me that I continued to let him down. I began to shut everyone out, including Mimi. I became increasing abusive to her. I would grab on her and throw her around frequently. I couldn't control anything else so I was going to control her.

After the semester was over, I rented an apartment with a friend from Chicago named Mundy. Mimi also moved in with us. I used some of my student loan money and purchased a pound of weed. Mundy and I sold marijuana to bring in extra cash. While pushing weed, I met some street boys from a nearby city called Peoria. Many of the guys were BD's. They were all tough and street hardened. Some were straight killers, so we all got along well.

Mundy and I sold a lot of weed. I didn't know if Mundy was smoking dope or tricking his money on women, but he was always broke. I had to stay on him for his portion of the bills. In order to help Mundy out, I gave him a pound of weed to sell on consignment. After a while, I noticed that Mundy wasn't staying at the apartment.

For over a month, I called Mundy on his cell phone, in attempts to retrieve my cut of the weed money. Mundy was spotted all over campus. It was obvious that he was avoiding me. I put out the word for whoever saw Mundy to contact me. A few weeks later, one of my friends named Ed called me. He told me that he had Mundy in front of the student center. Ed was a taller black male who looked like he was genetically engineered. Saying he was muscular was like saying the Statue of Liberty was tall. His muscles had muscles. His eyelids had muscles! Ed was known for annihilating men on campus. He was not to be messed with.

As I arrived at the student center, I saw Ed. Ed was forcibly holding Mundy on the sidewalk. If campus police would have seen us, they probably would have charged both of us with kidnapping Mundy. As I approached the two, Mundy exclaimed, "Man! I don't have your money so just go ahead and kill me!" I replied, "Fool! I know you mother! You have been watching too many mafia movies! I should tell her what you did and get us both in trouble!" Ed interjected, "You want me to fuck him up?" I gave Ed a brotherly hug and told him to let Mundy go. Mundy would have to get his weed from someone else.

It was mid fall of 1998. Mundy frantically rushed into our apartment. Before I could greet him, Mundy ran past me into his room, and closed the door behind him. Before I had a chance to ask what was going on, I heard a knock at the door. I opened the door to find a short and slender, black male looking very upset. He had a semi-automatic pistol tucked in the front of his pants.

The man identified himself as Peanut. He told me that he was about to shoot Mundy for ripping him off. Why does this sound familiar? Mundy ripped me off first. Plus, he hadn't washed dishes in weeks. If anybody was going to shoot him, it was going to me. Peanut said Mundy took dope to sell and never paid him back. As Peanut attempted to push past me, I blocked his path. Peanut grabbed the handle of his gun and yelled, "Nigga move out of my way!" I politely and forcefully told him, "You cannot come into my apartment to do anything! I am trying to change my life. I don't want any problems with you. You don't have the skills or the toughness to stop me at this close of a distance. If what you say is true, then you will have to take care of Mundy outside of my apartment."

I kept my eyes on his gun. I was prepared to take the gun from Peanut if he attempted to shoot me. Peanut replied, "I know who you are. I don't have a problem with you. I will respect your home, but that nigga is dead!" I shook Peanut's hand to make our words our bond. After closing the door, I went to Mundy's room to inform him that the coast was clear and that he had to move out. I never associated with Mundy again.

Having Mimi at home was not enough. I wasn't aware of it at the time, but I was using her. I knew I would never marry her, but I allowed us to live a married lifestyle. I needed a woman to be in my bed when it was time to sleep. I wanted a sex partner that was disease free. She was pretty and loyal but she was not the woman of my dreams.

Mimi knew I cheated on her. I believe she was patiently waiting to see if I could change. A few weeks later, I had a party at my apartment. Mimi stayed downstairs. She really didn't care for the guys I affiliated with. All my guys were upstairs in a spare bedroom. A girl came with them. One by one all of my guys departed. After a while the only people left were the lone lady and me. I locked the door and turned up the music. We ended up having sex right there in the spare bedroom!

I crept down the stairs to let the girl out of the back door, only to find Mimi on the couch crying. I ushered the girl out of the back door so I could tend to Mimi. I never wanted to hurt Mimi. I needed professional counseling. I had issues that were consuming my ability to become a better man. I needed more time with a good father figure to undo all of the negative traits I inherited back home.

After the indiscretion in our apartment, Mimi became more combative. She would physically fight me at the drop of a dime. A few times Mimi attacked me with weapons. After a big fight, we would make up with great sex. That routine never allowed us to address the complications and roadblocks in our relationship. We kept on with the makeup to break up dance for months.

It was late fall of 1998. Mimi came to me with a plan to purchase some clothes from the department store where she worked. Mimi was a cashier at Stein Mart. She said her coworkers would let their boyfriends buy clothing, but only scan a pair of socks. The next day I purchased three pair of Hilfiger pants with matching shirts. I grabbed a pair of socks so she could scan them of the clothing items. I had $300 worth of clothes and I only spent $25. As I was walking out of the door, security stopped me. Come to find out, the store was on to the scheme that their employees were pulling. The security guard asked to see my receipt and compared it to the items.

After an obvious discrepancy, I was taken to the back of the store and awaited police. Mimi and I were charged with retail theft over $250, which was a felony. It seemed that I couldn't stay out of trouble. I tried calling Robert but my mother kept intercepting the phone calls. I finally had to inform my mother that I was arrested again. My mother yelled, "You're gonna have to figure it out!" and hung up the phone. For once, my mother was right. I hadn't even settled the first felony and now I am fighting another.

I bonded out of jail with Mimi and returned home. Shortly after arriving at our apartment the phone rang. It was my father. How did he get my number? We didn't even talk. My father yelled, "You're down there fucking up? You are doing illegal shit again! What is wrong with you?" I replied, "You are one to talk! Not only were you abusive, but I can recall you doing illegal shit too! I remember the weed in our house! I remember the cocaine parties! You are no better than me!" My father yelled, "Who are you to judge me?" and hung up. Two minutes later my father called me back. This time he was much calmer. My father asked, "Can I claim you on my taxes this year?" I told him no and he yelled, "Well the law says I can do it so I am!" and hung up the phone again.

I knew what I wanted out of life. I knew that I wanted to grow to be just like Robert. My roadblock was that I didn't have enough positive examples in my lifetime to know how to properly achieve it. Up until college I lived life by a simple creed; "*Test me and we will be fighting. I don't care if it is one or one hundred, I am fighting! And if I am willing to fight over it, I am ready to kill over it!*" Robert was a real man. I looked up to him. He took care of me like I was his own. It should be easy to love your own kids. I was not of Robert's blood, but he gave me unconditional love anyway.

I focused hard on living right. I didn't go out to party. I ended up becoming a Supervisor at the APAC telemarketing firm. In a short period of time I ended up becoming one of the top supervisors in the nation. Within months, I was travelling with a team, to other APAC facilities, training their supervisors.

I successfully managed good grades in college as well. Dexter claimed to be tired of my father's tyrannical ways. He moved into my apartment and I even got him a job at my firm. I noticed my brother was different, but in a negative way. The first day my brother was at my apartment, he decided to go to a college campus party. It was around 2am on a work night when my brother frantically called, "About twenty niggas is trying to beat me up! Hurry up and get down here!" I asked, "What did you do?" Dexter screamed, "Nothing, they started fucking with me for no reason…hurry!" I told Dexter that I was on my way. Before I fully hung up the phone I heard Dexter yell, "My brother is coming! Now we will see what's up!"

I jumped into the car, ran every red light, and raced to the party. I saw Dexter standing in the parking lot. I jumped out of the car. Dexter rushed towards the crowd of guys yelling; "Now my brother is here! Talk shit now!" I aggressively walked towards the group attempting to harm my brother. One of the guys in the group recognized me and approached me. He told me that my brother insulted the group. Dexter was yelling profanities and calling them homosexuals. Dexter, as it turned out, was instigating with them. I snatched my brother up and chastised him all the way home.

It seemed like everyday someone told me of different instances where my brother would drop his pants to the ground, and expose his thong bikini. Upon exposing his male ass, with a string separating his cheeks, my brother would then pop his booty like a girl. What the hell was going on with my brother?

I kept talking to my brother, but to no avail. Dexter started smoking weed with the losers on campus. He also took my car when I was sleep and crashed it. Instead of telling me, the weasel parked the car like nothing happened. Dexter frequently called me a lame because I chose to work and go to school.

There was an individual who I knew through prior drug deals. We called him Face. He had a few girls that he would pimp out to his friends for free. One evening, Face, approached me and a group of my friends. He asked if any of us wanted a blow job from one of his girls. Of course I declined the offer. My friends declined as well. Dexter quickly leaped at the offer. We left Dexter to pursue more disease free ways of enjoying the night.

The next morning Face, who just previously offered us a gratuitous blowjob, was at my front door. He told me that my brother had raped his girl! In any other instance I would have believed Dexter's accuser, but this was a slutty female who sucked his dick. She had sex with anyone she was told to. How could he possibly rape her? Face and I went to talk to the lady. She was a slender, run down white lady in her mid-twenties. She told me that she did give Dexter a blowjob. In the middle of his free suck session, she claimed my brother yelled, "I can't take it!" and started taking off all of his clothes. She said Dexter pushed her flat on the bed and tried to undress her. She said that on several occasions she told him to stop. She claimed Dexter held her down and without a condom, forced his penis inside of her. This lady is a whore. She has to be lying…right?

Next, Face and I approached Dexter with the accusations. Dexter was caught red handed. He never denied any of it. His only reply was, "Man! I was too horny…I had to fuck her!" I yelled, "You fucking raped the lady!" What if she called the cops? He replied, "She's a hoe! She wasn't going to call the cops!" I couldn't believe the words that were coming out of my brother's mouth.

To make matters worse, less than a month of being hired at my firm, Dexter did the unthinkable. My brother came to work, broke into the firm's vending machine, and robbed it. After hijacking the spoils, Dexter left his shift early to smoke weed. I couldn't take it anymore. It was hard enough trying to get my life straight. I loved Dexter but I had to send him back to his father.

It was a lot of stress with school and work, but I was doing well. I had a sense of pride that was previously unimagined. I had to call and give Robert the great update. I called Robert constantly. My mother kept intercepting his phone calls. I assured her that I didn't need money and that I just wanted to talk to 'my father'. She intercepted his calls for months. Every time I called, my mother gave me a different excuse. It seemed like she had his cell phone all the time.

After months of being blown off, I called Robert's cell phone. I wasn't going to get off the phone until I talked to Robert. After my mother gave me some excuse, I yelled, "I want to speak to Robert now! Don't give me any more excuses, let me speak to him!" There was a brief pause. My mother's voice started to shake. She was crying. I didn't mean to hurt her feelings; I just want to talk to 'my dad'. My mother sobbingly replied, "Baby…Robert is dead! He died of cancer a while ago!" I knew why she did it. Robert probably left me some money. Anything that was left to me, my mother was going to inject into her veins. I didn't even get a chance to be there for him in his time of need. I never got a chance to let him know everything was going to be ok. I never got a chance to give him one final hug.

I never got to know my mother. She left too early for me to love her. Without any emotions, it is hard to hate someone. No! I didn't hate her. But now she was nobody to me. I politely and calmly replied, "You robbed me of a chance to be with my dad when he was dying. I loved him more than anything in this world. I never wanted anything from him. I know you are going to spend anything he left for me. I hope it was worth it because you died right along with him!" I hung up the phone only to realize that I was alone. I was more than depressed, I was dead inside. I put my fist through a wall to ease the pain.

Robert's death changed me for the worse. I became volatile. I lost my supervisory job at APAC by pushing an insubordinate employee out of my face. I didn't want to live anymore. I never shared that feeling anyone. I held it inside. But that type of pressure you have to release. I was a ticking time bomb. I started going to campus parties to mask my pain. In those parties, I ran into the angry drunk who wanted to test their pugilistic skills against the muscle bound athlete. If it was a fight someone wanted, it was a fight they would receive.

I would fight one guy or a group of men. I never let my friends help me. My loss of Robert left me numb. That numbness allowed me to fight with a reckless abandon that prevented me from feeling pain. I fought so much that when I entered a college party, the smart people would leave. I was getting arrested almost every other week. I was being arrested for everything from aggravated battery to obstruction of justice. I had a suspended driver's license but I continued to drive. At any given time, I was fighting three or four charges at a time.

But all that fighting will catch up to you…you can't win them all. It was the winter of my junior year. I went to a frat party. I was walking through the crowd when became dizzy. I thought that someone dancing accidentally elbowed me. I turned around to discover a man withdrawing his arm from the haymaker he landed to my temple. He retreated in fear because I was still standing after his punch. The guy hastily retreated to what the police report noted as fifty fraternity members.

The way his fraternity approached me, I knew that they were gearing up to cause me bodily harm. They wanted to fight me in the worst way. Even I can't take on that many guys. I retreated to gather my friends. It was seven of us total. Two of them were not fighters, but they would blow your brains out in a heartbeat. We approached the fraternity members. They attempted to surround us, not knowing the mortal danger they were in.

My friends didn't want to talk. They wanted people hurt. Something in me wanted different. I believe that was Robert talking to me. I backed my guys down. I made them stay calm. The guy who hit me was hiding like a coward behind his fraternity. I didn't recognize him at the time. But we had a previous altercation at another college party that left him sleeping on the concrete. As I attempted to diffuse the situation my friend, Hendo, decided to retaliate. He landed a haymaker to my cowering attacker's face. The punch was as loud as it was hard. Now the guy, who I had previously left sleeping on the concrete, was once again unconscious on the dance floor.

Security and police rushed the scene. Because of my violent history, I was the only individual detained. I was arrested for aggravated battery and obstruction of justice. I told the officers that I was not the one who punched the guy. The officers tried to get me to divulge who threw the punch. I was incapable of telling on a friend. With no one else to arrest for the crime, I was charged for it. The judge looked over my criminal record and my outstanding charges. I was informed that if I was found guilty on all charges I could face twelve years. The prosecutor told me that she took favor upon college students. She told me that I could get a lesser sentence if I informed her who actually committed the battery. I told her that I would only prove my innocence, not someone else's guilt.

If I plea bargained, the prosecutor was willing to offer me seven years in prison. I couldn't do seven years in prison! I decided to plead guilty, but I didn't agree to the seven year prison term. I left my fate up to a judge. In my most dire state, I had a moment of clarity. I knew what I wanted out of life. I also knew that I didn't want any more trouble.

I finally went before a judge for sentencing. Given my lengthy criminal history, the judge asked me give a reason why I shouldn't be sentenced to the maximum penalty. I paused to think for a moment. For once I was truly thinking about my life in its entirety. My reply was simple, "I don't want any more trouble, Your Honor." The judge glared at me for a long time and replied, "Given your record, how can I know this for sure?" As the judge sternly stared down upon me, I felt a sensation come over me. Robert was in that courtroom with me.

I replied in a way that I knew would make Robert proud. I decided to become a man and put all childish ways behind me. I said, "This is how you will know I am done with crime for good, Your Honor; while I was in high school, I almost killed a toddler in a drug deal gone bad. Those actions still torment me. I snatched my girlfriend around. I told myself that I wasn't abusing her because I wasn't actually striking her. But that was an excuse. I won't make any more excuses. I've been involved in several other fights that I have never been charged for. I have been driving, using a fake I.D. that my brother gave me. Today is the last day I will sneak and drive on a suspended license. I will surrender the fake driver's license I have on my person right now. I have accepted the victim role for too long. But I am a survivor. I am currently enrolled at Illinois State University. And I will become something of myself!"

The judge's reaction was one of shock and disbelief. I didn't get sentenced to the twelve year maximum sentence. I didn't get the seven year deal either. The judged sentenced me to ninety days in jail. He also stayed my jail time until the summer, so I didn't miss any of my college classes. I had to actually serve forty-five days in jail.

Life was still blurry, but that moment of clarity was priceless. That semester brought a lot of changes. Mimi and I got into an argument. During the argument, Mimi hit me in my head with a metal object. I was tired of fighting. I ended the relationship with Mimi. I told her to move out. There was many a night where I yearned for Mimi to lay next to me. A few times I tried to reopen our sexual past, but she declined. Without Mimi to help ease my financial load, I grew broke. A pawned several of my pricey items just to buy food. I was in a state of destitution, but I would never return to selling drugs or armed robbery. I didn't want welfare or any government aid.

I worked two part time jobs to make ends meet. I scraped and clawed until I found a good paying job. I became a union Laborer and made a decent salary. I paid off all my court expenses and got my life on track. I eventually became a foreman. It took a little while longer because of work, but I obtained my Bachelor's from Illinois State. I made a good name for myself in the union. I started to like the reflection in the mirror.

It's amazing how living a positive life opens the door to positive individuals. One evening I was driving to my apartment. I had to pass by Illinois State to get home. I noticed a lady with a little baby at the campus bus stop. I rolled down my window and shouted, "The buses aren't running anymore!" Something inside of me caused me to turn around to offer the lady and her child a ride. While driving her home, we both engaged in small talk. The lady informed me that she was a student at Illinois State and that she was from Chicago.

I told the female passenger that I too was from Chicago. I went on to inform her that I graduated from Simeon Vocational High School. The lady was surprised to hear that. She told me that her father had worked for Simeon for years. "What's your father's name?" I asked. She told me that her father's name was Shareef. I yelled, "Shareef is your father! Your dad is a great man! What a small world. He literally saved my life when some guys were about to shoot me!" I gave the lady my phone number and told her, "Anytime you need a ride, I want you to call me. You have a chauffeur for life."

Three years went past fast. I was enjoying life. I had a reputation for being a hard worker in my union. I had a sense of freedom, peace, and pride that I thought never was attainable. Those three years of peace were about to be disturbed. I received a phone call at my apartment. After picking up the phone, a male voice on the other line said, "This is your father." I interrupted, "How did you get my number? Why are you calling me?" My father calmly stated, "I know, I know. I had been following you. I noticed that you graduated from Illinois State University. I also know that you are a foreman in construction now. I am CEO of my own land development firm now. I was calling to see if you are happy with your job."

I told my father that I was happy with my occupation only to have him to continue talking. My father replied, "I could use a man of your caliber, experience, fortitude, and integrity." I responded, "Thank you but I am going to stay where I am." Before I could get off the phone my father blurted out, "Do you know how to perform demographic studies?" I replied, "That is a component of construction." He said, "I don't have anyone in my firm who can do that. I am willing to pay you $100,000 a year for your expertise. I am building a mall in one of the neighboring cities." That was more money that I have ever made.

I figured my father was attempting to make up for all the abusive acts. I replied, "$100,000 is a lot of money. Let me give my company a fair two weeks' notice." My father interrupted, "The only thing is that I need you to start tomorrow." For that type of money…screw it!

I didn't have time to make living arrangements so my father informed me that I could live with him until I found a place. While at was at my father's house, I noticed Dexter was less than happy to see me. As a matter of fact, Dexter seemed to be upset with me being temporarily in their home. My attempts at striking up a conversation with Dexter resulted in very curt responses. Dexter walked up to his room. I went to my brother's room to talk to him, but he was being so rude. While in his room, I bent down to pick a cd off of his floor.

As I was picking the cd up, my brother attempted to snatch it. I gripped the cd tight, which prevented Dexter from yanking it out of my hand. This visibly upset him. Dexter then yelled, "Daddy!" Our father flew upstairs to see what the commotion was. When our father entered the room my brother yelled, "Tell him to give me my cd!" I laughed while I explained how my brother was acting. Dexter in return yelled, "**I will grab my shotgun and shoot you in the face!**"

I never met anyone dumb enough to threaten to take my life. I was shocked at the remark. I calmly looked my brother into his eyes and said, "Remember who you are talking to. Your father won't be able to help you with this one!" My father looked at my brother and said, "That was uncalled for!" Dexter then started to cry and said, "I feel like I am the black sheep in this family!" What was wrong with him? I had no time to worry about my brother's childish acts. I got right to work. I compiled information for my demographical research to submit to my father. If I can recall, the site of the project was in the city of Matteson, Illinois. I spent weeks in the library. I studied public records and then compared my finding to similar cities in the U.S. I typed up my report and submitted my findings to my father. My father informed me that we would have a meeting with the mayor and some lenders in the weeks to come.

I had been at my father's house for almost three months without a single payment. I asked him about my pay periods. My father asked me to hold off until his grant came through. He would pay me all my back pay after he received his funding. I thought this to be weird but I agreed. Finally we went before the Matteson board. We talked to the members of the board and I presented my findings. It seemed like I was the only one prepared. I was a little confused.

After the meeting, a member of the board approached me. He said my presentation was splendid. He also advised me that I was wasting my time. He told me in confidence that my father was wasting everyone's time. He showed me paperwork that proved my father assembled this meeting without a single lending prospect. He also showed me how my father omitted certain steps. Basically, everything we did was for show. My father wasn't even remotely close to building a mall.

As soon as we arrived at my father's house, I pulled my father to the side. I informed him of the steps he failed to complete in the process of building on the site. I pointed out to him that he lied about having possible lenders. My father yelled, "You gonna tell me how to do my job? You need to leave my house before I get my shotgun!" While he was in route to retrieving his shotgun I replied, "Get what you want. But you are going to pay me before I leave this house for my three months of service. At $100,000 a year, you owe me $25,000." He stopped and said "I don't have that." He wrote me out a check for $500. I took the miniscule check and departed. I left my stable job because my father lied. My father was still a habitual liar. I wasn't bitter…I was smarter.

BAD NEWS WOO

I was weary. I needed a break. I decided to take a trip to Los Angeles, to visit a cousin on my father's side. I never met her before. Her name was Blondie. Blondie was full of life and energy. She was a kind of weird, which made me a little bit uncomfortable. Blondie was tall. She had a short haircut that was dyed blonde. She had no problems speaking about her sex life. Even worse, Blondie had no problems getting naked in front of me! I didn't know if it was her or the California way.

Blondie contacted her girlfriends. They decided to take me club hopping. One of her friends had long black hair, a tiny waist, and a big butt. She wasn't that pretty, but she possessed my Achilles heel; a small waist and a big booty. This lady went by the moniker, Woo. Woo and I flirted with each other. I became sexually intimate with, Woo. I flew back to California to visit her. Woo visited me in Illinois a few times as well. It was nothing serious at all. It was fun, since I wasn't in a relationship.

Even though she didn't look like it, Woo was about ten years older than me. Woo had no job and no intentions on working. She was in her mid-thirties and living with her parents. She was a high school dropout who eventually obtained her GED. The only good thing was that she had no kids to imitate her lazy lifestyle. Woo informed me that she had only dated drug dealers. She was used to her men giving her allowances. Her only duties were to satisfy her man sexually and shopping. She was someone to play with, not to settle down and have children with. Besides, Woo told me she was incapable of having children. I wanted children when I got married.

On a construction detail at a Dick's Sporting Store, I was injured. I tripped over some debris and tore cartilage in my knee. I was incapacitated and needed knee surgery. Before I was scheduled to have my surgery, Woo informed me that her father kicked her out of the house. She claimed she had nowhere to go. I figured she could help me post-surgery and serve as my sexual ambassador. I was never going to settle down with Woo. We could, however, help each other out, and have fun for a while. I told her that she could stay with me. That decision would be one of the worst decisions of my life.

Woo moved into my apartment a few weeks before my surgery. Initially everything went smooth. Woo made the meals. She cleaned the apartment. She made sure that I was taken care of sexually. After the operation, things started to change. Woo started smoking cigarettes and weed. I never smoked anything and I would never live with a woman who smoked. Before Woo arrived, we had a conversation. I told her what I would not put up with in my home. Smoking was high on that list. Woo lied and said that she didn't smoke. Woo started talking on the phone at all times of the night to her friends in California. I couldn't get a good night's sleep. My mind was made up; Woo would have to find somewhere else to stay.

I was healing from my operation. My leg was elevated and being iced. I decided to be upfront with Woo. I told her that the living situation was not working out. I gave her a few weeks to find living arrangements back in California. I told her I would buy her ticket back to Los Angeles. Woo became enraged. She kicked me off the bed. She then jumped over the bed on top of my knee. She grabbed my injured knee and began twisting my leg at the ankle. I attempted to counter possible damage to my knee by using my hands to twist my leg in the opposite direction. I was helpless and screaming in pain. This lady was crazy! I used my good leg to kick her off of my injured knee. I hobble in pain back to the bed. Woo spent the next few weeks of my recuperation sucking and fucking. Me being a dumb male, I took every payment.

As soon as I was able to walk and properly defend myself, I told Woo that she had a few weeks to get her affairs in order, and then she would have to move out. Woo coldly responded, "I have been here a month. By Illinois law, I have established residency here. Neither you nor the cops can force me to move out!" Shit! I am a criminal justice major, so I knew that to be correct. I had no recourse to force her out. I moved all my belongings in the spare bedroom and attempted to buy my time. I had three months left on my lease, and then I would move. She would have to figure it out from there. Woo knew I was done with her, so she became increasingly violent. She would often hit, slap, or punch me. I felt trapped.

After a while, my emotions got the best of me, and I started retaliating. If she hit me, I would throw her down. If she punched me, I would grab her by the throat. The problem was retaliating didn't stop the violence. Woo wanted to fight. It became a cycle of violence; we would fight back and forth for minutes.

I was dating other women, so I used those women to stay away from the apartment. Being away from Woo made her even more insecure, which in turn made her even more violent. The more violent she became, the more violent I reacted, under the misguided notions of self-defense. My lack of personal development didn't allow me to see that I had other options. I had become a naive participant in the cycle of violence.

I knew that I was selling myself short with Woo. I wanted better. I had to change my life to get better. I devised a plan to get better out of my life. I applied to be an electrician's apprentice at the electrician's union. The pay was way better and the work was less labor intense. After testing, and an interview, I was accepted into the apprenticeship. If Robert could see me now; he would be so proud of me. But I had to get Woo out of my life. She wouldn't leave the apartment, so I had to move.

Three months passed and I had clandestinely secured another apartment. While Woo was out of the apartment, my friends helped me to move. I left her half of the furniture and I even left her one of my cars. Later I ended up retrieving the car I left Woo. She didn't want to drive the car. She was upset that I didn't leave my new car for her to drive.

I don't know how, but Woo found my new apartment, and came to visit me. I noticed that she was driving a blue Jaguar. She wanted to come in and have sex. I respectfully refused her. She responded by landing a punch to my face. She walked to her car shouting profanities at me. I knew she was going to get worse…but I never could imagine how much worse.

Woo called my cousin Blondie telling her half stories of fights and abuse. She made me look like I just threw her around for no reason. She told my cousin I was cheating on her, but never revealed our current standing. On several occasions my cousin left berating messages on my voicemail. I never made any attempts to enlighten my cousin. She could believe what she wanted. I didn't really know Blondie to care one way or another.

One day I received a phone call from Woo. She informed me that she had keyed my new car. I ran outside to look at my car. It was keyed on the driver's side from bumper to bumper. In my hastened rage I informed her that I was coming to her apartment. She was going to have to pay me for the vandalism or I was going to kick her ass. I arrived at her apartment and she was talking to Blondie. I calmly stated, "I need you to call your Jaguar driving pimp and pay me for my car!" She laughed at me. I pushed the button down on the receiver to hang up the phone.

Woo grabbed at the phone and said, "I'm calling the police!" I knocked the phone out of her hand and replied, "Call whoever the fuck you want after you pay for my car!" I grabbed her by her throat and pushed her against the wall. I yelled, "You're going to pay to fix my car or I'm going to fuck you up!" There was a knock at the door. Woo started crying loudly. I know that knock! It was the police. Blondie called the cops and told them she heard me beating Woo. But that was impossible. When I hung up the phone we weren't even arguing. I can't believe what is going on. I wasn't sure if this was a coordinated setup or if my cousin acted alone. I was arrested and charged with domestic battery, false imprisonment, and interfering with a police call.

GROUNDED

Sadly, I was in a place that I knew all too well. I was in a place I said I would never visit again. I spent my birthday in jail. This was a new low. I was trying so hard to live right. Woo was bent on using me to take care of her. If I was not going to be with her, then she was hell bent on causing me harm. I had to find a way to persuade Woo not to testify. After I bonded out of jail, I contacted Woo. I had court orders not to contact her, but I was desperate. I bought her groceries. I told her I loved her. I cooked for her. I even had sex with her once. Woo agreed not to testify under the premise that we were going to be together. She said I had to move back in with her.

The state's attorney, however, had more than enough evidence to charge me. I was found guilty of battery and was sentenced to ninety days in jail with two years of probation. When I get out of jail, I will never have to see her ass again. I wouldn't care if she blew up my car. I would simply call the police. While I was serving my ninety day sentence, I had a visitor. It was Woo. What the hell did she want? If it wasn't for the monotony of jail, I would have refused her visit.

Woo initially tried to have small talk with me. I was very rude and abrupt with her. I told her to never visit me again. I indicated that I was done with her before she keyed my car. The whole time I was talking, Woo kept a halfcocked smile. Her smiled irritated me, so I stood up to gesture that our visit was over. As I was turning to leave, Woo said, "I haven't been feeling well. I have been really sick." While walking away and with my back to her, I replied, "Go to the doctor then!" Before I was out of hearing range Woo blurted out, "I did...I am pregnant."

I didn't believe her and I didn't trust her. She told me that she couldn't get pregnant. I purposely distorted my face to display that I didn't believe her. Woo fumbled through her purse and pulled out a white piece of paper. The paper had her name on it. One word in bold print stood out. That word was **'POSITIVE'**. She showed me the pregnancy test and the results from the doctor's visit. No way did I want a child by a deadbeat mother. For all I know, the father could have been the owner of the Jaguar that Woo drove.

When I was released from jail, I visited Woo. She was showing just a little. Damn! She was pregnant. My world just stopped. I was in disbelief. Woo was smiling and rubbing her stomach as if to say, "Yeah I got you now!" Out of frustration I said, "I want a paternity test!" Woo replied, "You can make a child but you cannot raise one? You are going to be just like your father!" Visibly upset I retorted, "I only had sex with you once!" You told me that doctors said that you were unable to get pregnant. What doctors did you go to? What test did they perform? Did a doctor really tell you that you were unable to conceive? Why would you lie about being able to get pregnant?" Woo snapped, "It doesn't matter now because I am pregnant with YOUR BABY!" I replied, "I don't know if the baby is mine. I had sex with you only once in the past year. And that was to get your crazy ass to drop the charges!" Woo yelled, "You are the only one I had sex with, Nigga!" I snapped back, "Yeah, right! Like a man is going to let you drive his Jaguar without you doing something sexual for him. I was born in a day, but not yesterday!"

But what if the baby was mine? No way was I going to be a deadbeat father. I was deeply saddened knowing that I could possibly have a baby by a woman, whom I had no aspirations on marrying. Nevertheless, if the child was mine, I had to step up. I didn't want my child to be born out of wedlock. I didn't want my kid to be born in anything but a house. I worked overtime to save enough money to purchase a house. I bought a seven year old house in a middle-middle class neighborhood. It had four bedrooms and 2 ½ bathrooms.

I loved the tri-level house and its finished basement. The backyard was huge and fenced in. The 2 ½ car garage was awesome as well. The backyard already had a swing and slide set. This would be a perfect house for my child. I allowed Woo to move in with me. We weren't close but we went through the motions well. I was a shell of a man. I was going to marry a woman that I didn't love, respect, or even like. My friends hated her. Four months later Woo brought a boy into the world. I was going to get a paternity test, but there was no need. This handsome newborn looked exactly like my father. It was no doubt that this little one was my son.

When the doctor attempted to hand our crying newborn to Woo, I snatched him into my arms. He immediately stopped crying. I held him close to my body. My whole life changed. I ignored the evil stares from the nurses while I stood in awe of my son. I started to think about my son's life. My son will be protected, loved, and raised unlike my father could have ever done. For the first time in my life, I was in love.

I kissed him over and over and over. I smelled his body, I rubbed his face. I knew then that I would never, ever go to jail again. I will lead by example. He deserves that type of father. As I held him he communicated to me by squeaking. That noise melted my heart. I gave him the moniker Squeak. I worked two jobs to take care of Squeak and his mother. I would race home and have my son in my arms the rest of the day. I even ate with Squeak in my arms.

With my beloved Squeak in my life I began to think about my mother and father. I recognized my mother for what she was…a woman who continued to victimize herself as she was victimized. I finally understood my father's plight. His baggage caused him to become stagnant. He didn't wish to grow to be abusive. In some way my father's past handicapped his ability to mature into a nonviolent patriarch. I no longer held on to apathy for my parents. I truly pitied them. I realized that I had a chance to be a far better parent than the ones I had. The energy I used to hate my father for his past transgressions was now used to become the best family man any woman could dream of. That epiphany marked the end of my nightmares…finally.

Woo still refused to work. I detested the fact that she didn't want to work. With my adjuration, she landed a job with a bank. It didn't last too long. I believe she got fired on purpose.

Woo started hitting me again, but I never allowed myself to get upset. I never laid a hand on her.

I was final fed up. I was killing myself to provide financial security for us and our child. I couldn't raise my son like this. He should grow in a home where his parents loved each other. I approached Woo and told her that I wasn't happy. I told her that I believed it would be more beneficial to our son if we lived separately. I told her that our son should have the opportunity to see both of us in positive and loving relationships. I told Woo that our son could have two good dads and two good moms, who could work together to raise him. I gave her a year to find a job and to find a place to live. To protect myself I had this agreement signed by the both of us and notarized. To show her I was serious, I slept in the basement downstairs. I still maintained an amicable friendship with Woo and we still did things together with Squeak.

Woo was initially fine with the arrangement. She started wearing lingerie all the time, in attempts to break my domestic celibacy. After months went past Woo started to realize that I was serious. Woo became more aggressive. She continually accused me of sleeping with multiple women. I always told her that it was none of her business. I could have told her the truth; that I wasn't sleeping with anyone. But I wanted to drive home the sentiments that the relationship was over. Every week I constantly reminded Woo that time was winding down and she had to find a place to live. I wasn't going to date until Woo moved out of the house.

It was the Saturday of July 4th weekend. Squeak was a year old. I was invited to a July 4th cookout. I had on a white tank top, white shorts and white Air Force Ones. As I dressed Squeak in similar garbs, Woo approached me. Woo angrily asked, "What bitch are you dressing my son up to look good for?" "Nobody", I replied. Woo insisted, "Don't be having bitches all in my son's face!" I replied, "We were invited to a cookout!" Woo interjected, "Well if someone invited my son, then I am going too!" I told Woo, "I am not there to meet any girls. I don't use my son to pick up women. If you want to come with us then get dressed."

Woo ran up the stairs to get ready. Twenty minutes later Woo walked down the stairs with skin tight, white jeans, a white blouse, and white high heels. She is not slick. She wanted to give the impression that we were a family. She wanted any pretty women at the cookout to see that I was in a relationship. It didn't matter. Next month in August Woo would be moving out of my house.

We arrived at the party and I was cheerfully greeted by everyone I knew. They all played with Squeak and attempted to be hospitable with Woo. At the party I saw one of the most beautiful women that I have ever seen. Her hair was brown with tan streaks and it was styled just above her shoulders. Her skin was light caramel and smooth. Her body was slim and accented by a nice summer's dress. She had on high heels and her demeanor was that of a classy lady. She actually seemed out of place at this cookout. She used Bible scriptures to drive home positive points during her conversation, and she kept a pleasant smile.

All of the guys at the cookout were drooling over her. I wasn't staring but I definitely checked her out. She paid none of the men any attention. As a matter of fact, she seemed to detest the lustful attention she was receiving from them. The host of the cookout introduced me to this beautiful lady. Her name was Carlotta. That was different type of name. She was born in Bloomington. After receiving her Masters, she ran a grant funded program in Chicago. Damn, what a catch. The host introduced me as Woo's husband. We weren't married…where in the hell did she get that impression from? I had no chance with her now. I greeted Carlotta and continued to enjoy the cookout. After leaving the cookout, I felt a little down. I returned home to remind Woo of our year move out agreement. She had less than a month before her move out date was reached.

The next day, the host of the cookout invited me over to indulge in leftovers. As I entered the house, I noticed Carlotta sitting on the couch, and stuffing soul food in her mouth. She might look all ladylike, but she eats like a lineman. I stayed there all day. I missed Squeak, but I enjoyed the vacation from the blood sucking, leach of a baby's mother. The night was fun. We played cards, watched television, and conversed.

I attempted to hold a conversation with Carlotta. She interrupted me to inform me that she does not flirt with married men. I told her that I have never been married. I informed her that currently I wasn't even in a relationship. Carlotta rolled her eyes and rudely initiated a conversation with the other ladies in the living room. I understood. Just the day before, I was with my son and the mother of my child dressed alike. Woo is slick and her plan worked. Carlotta continued her intellectual conversation with the ladies. I interrupted their conversation to expound upon what they were discussing.

While I was talking I made mention to a word that Carlotta was unfamiliar with. She sarcastically asked me what the word meant. The way Carlotta questioned me, alluded that I had made the word up, or used it incorrectly. I spelled the word, gave her the definition, and used the word in a sentence. She couldn't hide how I impressed her with my intellect. I gloated in the moment. I teasingly stated, "Yeah! This muscle bound, tattooed looking heathen has some brains!" Everyone in living room started to laugh, even Carlotta. She quickly snapped out of her laughter and returned to her look of disapproval with me. At least she started including me in the conversation. Slowly but surely, Carlotta started warming up to me.

Carlotta and I continued to talk into the night. One by one people from the cookout departed. Soon, it was just Carlotta and me on the couch. We talked about life, religion, the economy, food, and everything in between. This was the most stimulating conversation that I had ever had. I loved talking to this woman. I loved looking into Carlotta's beautiful face. Somehow or another, our conversation transitioned to my situation with Woo. She told me it sounded like a bunch of lies. I assured her my situation was a truthful nightmare. She had recently separated from the man she was involved with since she was fourteen. They had three younger sons together. She didn't look like she had any kids let alone three. At least they are with the same man.

Carlotta said that she was not with him anymore because he wasn't an involved parent and he started to take her for granted. We sat and talked on that couch until 5am. We agreed to stop talking to get some sleep for thirty minutes. We both had to go to work and she had to drive all the way back to Chicago.

Before I departed for work, I gave her my number so she could let me know that she arrived to Chicago safe. I told her that I loved our conversation and I would like to talk to her some more.

Carlotta called me to inform me that she had made it safe. I told her to call me so we could talk more. She told me of her reservations, seeing that I still lived with the mother of my child. I told Carlotta that I had done little in life to warrant trust, but if she gave me one chance, I would earn hers.

I developed an honest bond with Carlotta. We talked on the phone all day every day. She visited me in Bloomington every Thursday through Sunday. It was near the end of July when I met Carlotta's sons. We all hit it off immediately. They loved me. Their father was not actively involved in their life. This made her boys latch on to me even harder. I rode her sons on my motorcycle. We went to carnivals and out to eat. They loved having a man around to do guy things. I introduced Carlotta to Squeak. She watched over him like he was her child. That was when I knew she was the one.

Woo started snooping through my phone account to see if I was constantly communicating with someone. She discovered Carlotta's number throughout my call history. Woo gave me this warning, "Don't give up on us. You will regret it!" I respectfully reminded her of our agreement and walked to the kitchen.

Woo followed me to the kitchen to continue the discussion. She wasn't grasping the fact that she had to move out. She grabbed my penis, in hopes that I would acquiesce into a sexual interlude. We hadn't had sex since I moved to the basement almost a year before. I backed away from Woo while swatting her hand away. As I was telling her that I met someone, Woo fell to the ground. She was lying on her back in the kitchen. While on her back Woo questioned, "What happened? What did you do to me?" I feared for my safety. I knew I was about to go to jail for domestic violence again.

Out of panic, I immediately called Carlotta on the phone. I told her that Woo was on the ground but I never laid a hand on her. I told her that I believed Woo was trying to set me up. I called a friend to be a witness and to get me out of the house. Out of embarrassment that I had informed people of her plot, Woo got off the ground. Woo stated, "I wasn't going to tell the cops you hit me. I know you didn't hit me. I just passed out." I finally saw Woo's true mindset.

July was almost over. August was a few days away. I notified Woo that she had to have a plan to move out by the end of the month. When the end of the month arrived, I would learn firsthand of Woo's plan.

It was the first week of august. I was returning home from work. Woo was supposed to be moving on this day. When I pulled into my driveway, two sheriffs jumped out of their cars. They approached me with their weapons covered. They notified me that I had to leave my home by court order. When they handed me the order, I noticed it was an order of protection! In the order of protection I was ordered to surrender my house and one of my cars to Woo. The order specifically stated to give Woo the new car.

I was ordered to stay away from Woo and Squeak. Instead of moving out, Woo was plotting in the courthouse. Woo claimed that I molested my son, beat him, and tried to kill him in front of her. Woo also alleged that I beat her and held her captive in my house. This was really happening. The sheriffs allowed me five minutes to get my clothing for work only. I could not take any of my personal belonging because Woo misled the courts to believe we were married. The division of my personal belonging would be determined on a later court date.

I assured the sheriffs that this was a tactic by a lady who wanted to be provided for. I told the two sheriffs that I understood the terms of the order of protection for Squeak and Woo. I agreed to leave without any resistance if I could hug and kiss my son goodbye. They allowed. As I held Squeak, tears streamed down my face. I wasn't sure when I was going to see him again. He was a daddy's baby. He was my baby. Now a piece of paper signed by a judge mandated that I could no longer see my only child.

Woo was an older woman who was slick. She was in a league way above me. While I was working, she was plotting. While I was caring for our son, she was scheming. I didn't stand a chance. For the next five months, the only time I saw Squeak was in court. I had to pay the mortgage and for an apartment. I had to pay two utilities. I was hurt mentally, emotionally, and financially. I went into a mental state I thought I evolved from. I was going to kill Woo. There are so many deadbeat dads around. Why would Woo stop a good dad from seeing his son? I knew I would be the prime suspect if something happened to Woo, but I didn't care. She could not get away with this.

Then I thought about Robert. What would he think of what I was planning to do? Then I thought about Squeak. If I bring any harm against his mother, then I am no better than her. The courts eventually saw through Woo's actions and dropped the order of protections against her and Squeak. Woo was granted custody of Squeak, but I finally got visitation with my son. I was to be with my son on alternating weekends, summers, and holidays. This decision enraged Woo.

The first day I was with Squeak, all I did was hug him. I couldn't let him go. Squeak was noticeably sick, but I was too happy to see him to ponder on it much. I was still living in an apartment. Woo was still living rent free in my house, but I was the happiest man in the world. Squeak loved Carlotta and had a ball with her sons. Our families blended together perfectly. The next week I got Squeak, I remember him being sick again. The following time I received Squeak, he was sick as hell. What was going on? Every time I received my son he was sick. One of the last times that I had visitation with Squeak, he had hundreds of insect bites all over his body. I spent my weekend with my son in the emergency room. The emergency room doctor believed they were flea bites, but they couldn't say conclusively.

The courts finally allowed me to move back into my home. The judge ordered Woo to relinquish my car. When I retrieved my car, I was shocked. My new car was keyed on every part. The back seats were ripped out. The gas tank was glued shut. The seatbelts, visors, window controls, door controls, and the key holes were bonded with some type of industrial adhesive.

Upon arriving in my home, I discovered more unthinkable deeds. All the lights were on and the water was running. All my windows were gorilla glued. All of the electrical outlets had foreign objects gorilla glued inside of them. All of my ceiling fans were rendered inoperable. All my furniture, appliances, dishes, and clothing were gone. Someone decided to defecate on the floor of the main level bathroom. Someone also pissed all over the walls in that same bathroom. Woo left a photocopied picture of my face on the counter, where my appliances used to be. My lips on the photocopy were colored red. On top of the picture Woo wrote the caption, "You little Bitch! Look who looks like a bitch now!"

There were semen filled condoms strategically placed throughout my house. My washer, dryer, stove, and microwave were gone. She even sold my two dogs! I petitioned the courts to force her to retrieve my dogs. Woo sent a letter to the courts saying I only petitioned to move back into my home and I made no mention to keep my personal property inside of it. Nothing was hers to sell. She didn't buy a damn thing. What kind of psycho bitch sells a man's dogs? The worst part of Woo's vengeful act was that she took all the photos I had compiled of Squeak. I kept the pictures in a locked, fireproof safe. The safe was still in the room where my computer used to be. The safe's lock was broken and its contents emptied.

I filed a police report, and my homeowners insurance replaced everything. I had a house full of new clothes, furniture, dishes, computer, and appliances. I was given a lump sum to total out my car. I would have traded that all to have Squeak's pictures and my dogs back. Seeing that Woo was mentally unstable, I filed for sole custody of Squeak. The courts decided it was better for a child to live with his mother on public aid, in an apartment, versus living with his middle class father, in the house he was born in. I feared for my son. How could she be a good mother, yet be hell bent on destroying his father?

Carlotta decided to leave Chicago so that we could start a life together. Shortly after moving back into my house, the police approached me and Carlotta. A police sergeant informed us that a man was questioning my whereabouts, in attempts to shoot me. They had reason to believe that this man had an intimate relationship with Woo. The guy was only sixteen.

My life sounded like a movie. They assured me that the situation was under control and pleaded with me not to take matters into my own hand. I was in love and I had a family. I couldn't risk getting into trouble. I pressed the police to file charges against Woo for statutory rape. If I could prove she had an illegal sexual encounter with a teen, then I could get custody of Squeak for sure. The police informed me that they didn't have concrete evidence to charge Woo.

I had a devotion to Carlotta unlike any other. I wanted to keep a smile on her face. She only wanted the simple things, so it made it easy for me to give her more. She had a raggedy car, so I bought her a Cadillac Escalade for her birthday. I knew she was the woman that I could not live without. Lost in my whirlwind romance, I went to Kay's and purchased an engagement ring. The ring had a little less than a karat center stone with smaller, complimenting diamonds along the sides.

Carlotta was the only female in the house. With a man in the house taking over the parenting duties, Carlotta developed a diva complex. There were four males in the home, and we constantly got on her nerves. She would fuss at me because the boys peed on their toilet seats. She fussed when they rough housed. She would fuss if their rooms were dirty. When she fussed it humored me because she deserved a break.

It was the winter of 2006. The boys and I were rough housing. We were in middle of our free-for-all WrestleMania, when we became too loud for her liking. While the boys were cleaning up our mess, Carlotta relayed her displeasure with me. I pulled out the engagement ring and proposed. She immediately stopped fussing and started crying. I already had her ring sized, so it fit perfectly. That was the first, last, and only time I came out a victor in one of her fussing sprees. I spent a lot of money on her truck and the ring, so Carlotta and I clandestinely married in the courthouse.

My wife convinced me to introduce the boys to my father. She said that Squeak needed to know all of his family. The first time we brought our boys to meet my father, he was shocked. He knew I would never speak to him again. But there I was, at his house, with our kids. Dexter was obviously upset that I had decided to visit. He kept a slight frown on his face and barely even spoke.

My father interacted with all our boys. He was surprisingly pleasant. He picked up Squeak and Squeak started to cry. My father would beat us if we cried. My pulse was racing. If he even looked like he would hurt my son, I would have beaten him to death. My wife, sensing my escalating tension, gently caressed my back to calm me. Much to my surprise, my father patiently and gently coaxed Squeak until he was comfortable with him. He hugged our boys and interacted with them. This wasn't the woman and child beater that I grew to know.

    This man was surprisingly great with his grandkids. While visiting my father, he confided to me that I had a younger brother. His name was Ryan. He said Ryan was conceived while he was with Fran. He told me Ryan was a teenager. While my father told me of my new little brother, Dexter laughingly interjected, "Yeah but he is gay though." Our father shot Dexter a look of disapproval before continuing. He then called Ryan on the phone. After a short conversation, my father handed the phone to Dexter. Dexter and Ryan had a relationship, so they had a few laughs and then I received the phone.

    I introduced myself to Ryan. The conversation was devoid of emotion because I didn't know Ryan. After a few minutes I got off the phone. As soon as I hung up, Dexter was laughing and waiting on me to respond. Dexter then said, "I told you he was gay!" and began to laugh. I'll admit that Ryan did sound a bit effeminate. But, how masculine is a boy supposed to be after being raised by his mother? My father was not in his life.

    Before I left, my father hugged me goodbye. I returned my father's hug with an emotionless pat on the back and a smile. Floyd Butler had committed too many atrocities for us to ever have a loving relationship. Our relationship would be cordial at best. I would give him the chance to bond with his grandchildren. They could never be alone with him, but he would still get a chance to know them.

    It was late fall when my father and Dexter visited my home. I am sure Dexter didn't want to come with our father. Floyd Butler probably forced him to come. I was overwhelmed with custody hearings and my job. Carlotta had to work. I asked Dexter if he could watch my boys, while I ran some errands. I returned home to find my adult brother viewing pornographic material on a laptop with my sons around him.

    I was enraged at the fact that an adult would allow children to view sexually explicit material. I yelled, "What type of role model does this in front of kids?" Dexter said, "Why are you so upset? Calm down. You asked me to watch them. I couldn't help it. I was horny as hell, but I had to watch your kids!" Dexter was never allowed at my house again. After the internet porn episode with my brother, a friend called me to notify me that Dexter was on the Iowa sex offender's registry.

Out of concern, I called our father. He told me that Dexter attended a small college in Iowa. He said that Dexter had consensual sex with a lady. After the sexual interlude was over, Dexter dissed the girl, and she subsequently claimed rape. Our father assured me that Dexter didn't rape the lady, but he was only repeating the story that Dexter fed him. Evidently something happened because Dexter was found guilty for the sexual assault. I investigated on the internet to see Dexter's head shot on the Iowa's sex offender registry. The pattern for the Dexter was definitely established. I hope he gets the help he needs.

Around this time my sister Jen got into contact with me. Hearing Jen's voice was a true testament to God's power. She was doing very well. Jen was able to endure all that abuse, yet still become a functional member of society. Jen and her friend flew from California to visit my family and me. I was so happy to see her. We talked for hours. I hadn't seen my sister in years but we interacted like we lived our whole lives together.

Before Jen departed, she gave me Foxy's number. She told me that our beloved Foxy was in good health. I never thought I would get a chance to hear Foxy's voice again. I called Foxy to catch up. Foxy was older and wasn't a big fan of long conversations. She was happy to hear from me. I told Foxy about my wife and kids and she asked for a picture.

Before I got off the phone Foxy, asked me if Dexter had given me my bond. The bond was started for me when I was born. There were two bonds. One was for my brother, Dexter, and the other one was for me. That was weird. Dexter never mentioned anything about a bond to me. After getting off the phone with Foxy, I called Dexter. I asked Dexter about a bond that was supposedly sent to me. Initially he hurried off the phone. Later, he admitted to receiving his bond, but adamantly denied ever receiving mine. Dexter said Foxy was senile and dismissed her claim. I just got off the phone with Foxy. She was every bit in her right mind. My wife made a good point. She told me that it didn't matter who possessed my bond. An individual would need picture identification to cash it. This matter would come to light later on.

Woo was livid over the fact that Squeak preferred being with us over being with her. This frustration led Woo to petition the courts to allow her to move back to California. She detailed to the judge how she would get on Section 8 and food stamps and raise Squeak. No way would the courts allow this. I know she is the mother, but I was a working member of society.

A mother begging for handouts is not a stable guardian for a child. It could send the wrong message to the children about being productive members of society. Surprisingly, the judge granted Woo permission to move back to California. They detailed how I would get two weeks in the summer with Squeak. I would also get alternating Christmases. I was designated an hour on Wednesdays to talk to my son. I had to pay half of the plane tickets, which was not counted towards my child support payment. Boy was I lucky…not! Woo and Squeak moved to California.

It would be impossible to build a relationship with my son on such little quality time. Even though there was a standing court order, Woo refused to send Squeak for my two week visitation. I had to petition to the judge twice. Woo finally relented because the courts detailed possible punishments associated with interfering with my visits. Woo informed me the night before the flight that Squeak would be flying into Chicago. She flew with him.

Woo harassed me the whole time I was in the airport. For over an hour, Woo played phone tag and stayed in an area of the airport that I was unable to access. I had to call the airport police to force her to hand over Squeak. Three days into our reunion with Squeak, I get a call from Woo. Woo said, "Umm…Squeak has something in his ear! I had been calling your phone to tell you that. If you don't take him to the emergency room now, I am going to inform the courts that you are abusing my son!" I snapped, "Why didn't you tell me this when you handed Squeak off to me? I only have one missed call from you. Why didn't you leave a voicemail about this?" Woo interrupted, "Whatever! Take care of it or I am going to have you arrested for child abuse!" Woo hung up the phone. I informed my wife of the weird conversation I just had with Squeak's mother. We looked into both of his ears, but we couldn't see anything.

We decided to take Squeak to the emergency room to protect ourselves. The emergency room doctor called a specialist for an object lodged into the furthest point of Squeak's ear. A children's advocate questioned me to the specifics of Squeak's accident. The doctor assured me that my three year old son was incapable of stuffing a new pencil eraser that far down his ear canal. I started to put it together; every time during my visitation my son was sick. I started to believe Woo had some form of Munchausen's syndrome. I started to fear for Squeak's safety.

It was obvious that she would go to any length to hurt me...even if that meant bringing harm to her own child. After I sent Squeak back to California, Woo refused to let me talk to Squeak, even though it was court ordered. It was only for one hour a week. How selfish can his mother be? I continued to pay child support even though I knew all the money wasn't being spent on Squeak. I continued calling on my court scheduled Wednesdays for almost a year. A little after that, I decided to stop calling. I would not give Woo the satisfaction of denying me to talk with my son.

I sadly understood that Woo was hurting Squeak by her actions. When my summer visitation arrived, Woo refused so send Squeak. The courts informed me that they were unable to force Woo to send Squeak. They could charge her with interference of child visitation, but she could only be arrested for it if she came back to Illinois. Besides, she was the custodial parent. I started to wonder how bad Squeak would be injured if she was forced to send him again. I love my son with every fiber of my being, but I can't be the catalyst for more injuries to him. I thought it was better to not press the issue. One day, we will talk, and I will explain everything. One day I will get the chance to tell him that I love him with all my heart. I will tell him how I held him when he was born. I would tell him stories how I rode him on my motorcycle when he was one. I will tell him that I carry him in my heart, wherever I go.

Squeak would be glad to find out that Carlotta and I are still married. About four years after we married, we gave Squeak a little brother. His name is PJ. The two looked alike when they were born. I'm in love, I'm married, I am happy, and I am a contributing member of society. This is where the book ends with 'Happily Ever After'…right? This couldn't be further from the truth!

MURDERER!

Ten days after PJ was born, I received a call at 2am. On the other line was a policeman. The officer told me that he was at the house of Floyd "Bullet" Butler. He notified me that a single shotgun blast decapitated my father. The officer went on to tell me that Floyd recently had double knee replacement. Apparently while my father was asleep on the couch, the perpetrator crawled on his hands and knee behind the couch. The killer then placed a pillow right above my father's head and shot him with a shotgun. Nothing was stolen or vandalized. It wasn't a robbery either.

    The officer recounted what information they gathered thus far. Around 1am Dexter and an alleged cousin discovered the headless body of our father. The officer queried me about this cousin, but I knew nothing about him. The officer told me that someone kicked in the back door. They believe this action was staged because there were only footprints entering the door. There were no footprints exiting the door. Plus, the backdoor was concealed. It was impossible to know there was a backdoor by a complete stranger, or even someone casing the house.

The officer said that someone tried to stage my father's headless body in a way that made it look like a suicide. The only problem was that the gun was missing. Lastly I was informed that Dexter was discovered as having his shoes untied. This was odd because allegedly, he just discovered the body from a night out. The officer put Dexter on the phone. Dexter sobbingly explained, "Dad was depressed by the pills he was taking. He decided to sleep on the couch. Before he went to sleep, Dad told me to bring him his shotgun. I told him no and I hid the shotgun in the closet. He's...he's dead!" Dexter went on to tell me that our father indicated to him that he was tired of his life, and therefore, probably killed himself. After Dexter finished talking I replied, "It will be ok. Don't stare at the body because it will stain your memory." Dexter handed the phone to a detective on the scene that I grew up with named Tony.

Tony: "Luther, are you there?"
Me: "Yeah Tony, how are you doing bruh?"
Tony: "Man Luther, come home! This doesn't look or sound like it was a suicide! The body looks a little staged. Man, come home! I know the past between you and your father, but the family is going to need you now!"
Me: "Okay. I will wake my family up right now."
Tony: "Man Luther...Your brother...it doesn't look good for..."
Me: "I already know! You don't have to say anymore! Thanks big bro!"

    Dexter told me that our father indicated to him that he was going to take his own life. The only problem with that story was a man wanting to die probably wouldn't get double knee replacement.

    Our father may have been in his seventies, but he was in great shape. Plus our father was terribly vain. By having a degree in criminal justice, I didn't need to be informed that whoever killed him probably was an acquaintance. Whoever killed our father was in the house when he went to sleep. The officer's vague questioning couldn't mask his belief that my brother and this mystery cousin were somehow involved. My wife and I took the two hour drive to Chicago early in the morning. During the drive, I called family members to question about this mystery cousin. I discovered that he was a family member on my mother's side. I was told the same thing by everyone I talked to. They told me that this cousin wasn't a good person to be around. They all said he was in and out of trouble and could be violent.

When I arrived at my father's house, I noticed a couple of weird coincidences. The first was that my sister Telly was already sitting at the table. How did her fat ass arrive way from Oklahoma before my wife and I did? Even the police questioned how she arrived so fast. Was she in on it? Was she covering for Dexter? The second oddity was the fact that my mother was sitting at the table as well.

My father literally grew to hate my mother. She was obviously still addicted to drugs. She looked terrible. She was definitely after all that she could get. Fran was quietly crying in my father's dining room. As Fran and my mother looked at my newborn, PJ, I began to open some drawers in a nightstand. The nightstand was against a wall in the dining room. The first drawer I opened had a duplicate state identification card in my name. I never applied for a duplicate id…so who did? At least I knew how my bond was cashed. Telly was sitting at our recently murdered father's dining table with Fran, Dexter, his girlfriend, my mother, older cousins, this mystery cousin, my nephew, some of Dexter's friends, and some street thugs who really had no reason to be there.

Everyone at the table began to talk about Floyd "Bullet" Butler's murder. Dexter initially told everyone in the house that our father committed suicide. I yelled out, "Bullshit! Floyd was vain as hell! A man who wants to kill himself doesn't opt to enhance his quality of life by getting double knee replacement!" The other family members shook their heads in agreement. Dexter then replied, "I think the pills might have depressed him." I snapped at Dexter, "Get the hell out of here!" Dexter sat quietly, with his head down, as if he was in deep thought. Telly immediately interjected, "Pills can make people act funny!" Nobody replied to her fat ass.

After a minute of silence Dexter exclaimed, "I know! I was into it with some niggas on the street. They probably killed Dad to get back at me…it was a hit!" I yelled out, "Get the fuck out of here! That is some shit you see in the movies! I am a street boy. If someone wants to get you, then they are going to get you. There would be no need to kill a fucking senior citizen!"

Telly immediately placed her arm around Dexter, as if to protect him from my verbal attack. Dexter then told everyone in the house that the killers were probably mobster hit men trying to stop our father from building a Casino in Las Vegas. Dexter said, "When the hit men kicked in the door, my father was on pain medication. The pain medication prevented him from hearing the door being kicked in." I am obviously irritated. I again yell out, "Get the fuck out of here! I have had a few knee operations. Pain medication helps you to sleep. It doesn't put you in a comatose state!"

Dexter retreated further into Telly's arms while Telly replied, "It is true. The pain medication stopped dad from waking up." I hated Telly with every fiber of my being. I looked her into her eyes and exclaimed, "Tell that bullshit to someone who isn't educated!" I later turned to Dexter and yelled, "If you discovered Floyd after returning from a night out, then why were your shoes untied?" Dexter yelled out some gibberish and returned to his silence. One of Dexter's unsavory looking friends callously blurted out, "Dexter, I know you are doing your family thing, but we got to go!" Did this man say we were doing our family thing? We were trying to figure out our father's murder. Dexter jumped up and hurried out of the door.

Dexter and his rugged looking friends all huddled outside near the garage. Then they all started getting into cars. As I continued to watch, I observed Dexter immerge from the garage with a big blue duffle bag. I ran outside to ask Dexter what was in a big blue bag. He told me that it was his personal guns. I asked, "Where you about to go with the bag?" Dexter said, "We are about to get into a shootout with some niggas! We are about to handle some business right now!" If I would have been thinking, I would have either taken the bag or called the cops. It could have been evidence in that bag. Dexter and some of his friends jumped into our father's car and sped off. When Dexter returned, he didn't have that duffle bag.

As soon as Dexter and his hooligans left, my nephew approached me. My nephew who was quietly crying said, "Dexter killed my granddad!" I asked him, "What makes you say that?" My nephew told me that he and Fran were with his granddad and Dexter. He said Dexter started cursing and yelling at his granddad. That was weird! He was cursing at Floyd Butler? Dexter was deathly afraid of his father. My nephew went on to say that his granddad had to take the verbal abuse because his operation left him incapacitated. My nephew and Fran left my incapacitated father around ten pm.

    As I was talking to my nephew, one of Dexter's high school friends approached me. He told me that he was positive that Dexter had killed our father. He told me days prior to the murder, my dad confided in him about Dexter. He told me that our father informed him that he was about to kick Dexter out. He said Floyd had become weary of Dexter's behavior. He claimed that our father disapproved of Dexter's new cohort…this mystery cousin. He told me that my father no longer wanted this cousin at his house. If he was no longer allowed at my father's house, then why was he showing up at our father's door with Dexter at 2am? Dexter has been cowardly his whole life. In my heart I knew he played a part in the murder, but I am sure he had help.

    I returned home to wrap my head around all that had transpired. I wasn't even settled into my home when I received a barrage of phone calls. My father's banks began to inquire to the oldest living child of our father. Telly misleading took the role as eldest sibling. This gave her control of our father's estate and a certain amount of money in his account. In the past Telly had been a homeless drug addict. Now she saw a financial means to an end. Telly was a little too anxious to gain control of the estate and his finances. Telly and Dexter both displayed anxiety when I was at our father's house. They might have believed that I would forcefully take control of our father's estate. None of them truly knew me.

    Telly's first move was a bold one; she moved her boyfriend and her kids into our father's house. Telly was one of many people that my father duped into believing that he was financially well off. I couldn't wait for reality to crash down on her phony leaching ass! In addition to Telly moving in, my drug addict of a mother moved her and her drug addict boyfriend into the house. The blood that soaked into the hardwood floors probably hadn't dried, and another grown man is sleeping in our father's bedroom. The scenario was more than sick, it was utterly disrespectful.

Evidently, this mystery cousin was laying his head at the house as well. Dexter felt the need to be surrounded by people at all times. Everybody had their hands out. The only one who didn't was me. I earned everything I had the right way. I wasn't going to compromise my integrity by accepting anything from anyone…let alone from someone whom I didn't respect. I was proud of the man I became. I truly liked what I saw when I looked into the mirror.

The lead detectives handling my father's murder drove two hours to ask me some questions. The first thing that the detectives informed me was that they had strong reason to believe that Dexter was involved with the murder. They went on to allude that they believed this cousin was involved as well. The detectives pointed out that Dexter informed them that he was a high ranking member of the Black Disciples.

Dexter told the detectives that our father's murder was a gang retaliation. Dexter, a high ranking BD…not! There was a reason that he neglected to tell that lie at the table. I could have called him on that lie easy. What high ranking member of a gang admits to such? They all want to stay under the radar. The detectives said they obtained a warrant to check Dexter's phone.

After the murder, Dexter sent some texts to his girlfriend. Some of the text alluded to putting away a shotgun. There was also a text which asked if he could trust her with his life. The detectives asked me about a will that was produced by my brother. The will was null and void because it was updated after my father's death. I hope this murder wasn't for money and his estate, because the world is about to find out how deceptive my father was. He was broke.

Within days of me having a candid conversation with my brother, classmates of Dexter began to call me. They told me that Dexter was upset over my questioning. They said Dexter was fuming and stated on more than one occasion that he had guys who could kill me. I didn't take it lightly because there was already one man dead. He would, however, have to try and kill me from behind. He didn't know people tough enough to attack me head on.

Out of the blue, Telly's daughter, Monique, called me from our father's house. My niece was frantic. She said she was too scared to live in the house. She said that this mystery cousin started getting high and punching holes in my father's house. She said he verbally made mention to the fact that he had no problem killing old people and children. Another one of Dexter's high school friends was at the house at the time. He was visiting from the military. Shocked by what he heard, he called me to inform me of this statement as well.

My niece went to her mom, Telly, and told her of her fears. Monique said Telly reacted by physically assaulting her. After the beating that removed handfuls of hair out her daughter's head, Telly kicked her daughter and her grandson out of the house. These events had more twists than a Lifetime Movie! I retrieved my niece and her son and sent them back to Oklahoma.

They held our father's funeral some days later. The memorial was held at the Simeon High School, where my father retired. A few minutes from the memorial, I received two separate phone calls. Both were from classmates of Dexter. Evidently Dexter had some guys at the funeral waiting for me to show up. They were openly looking to fight. I stepped on the gas. I couldn't get there fast enough. I was going knock out anyone disrespectful enough to fight me at my father's funeral. My wife quickly made point that I was a husband and a father. She gently told me that a real man is one that goes out of his way to keep harm away from his wife and kids. She was right. We were only a few miles from the memorial when we turned around to head back home.

Hundreds of kids, fellow teachers, family members, friends, and three of his children attended Floyd "Bullet" Butler's funeral. His students loved him. They all said that he was a kind, loving, and compassionate teacher. That is when I truly understood. I believe my father attempted to make amends for being abusive by being a good mentor to his students. The parental system failed my father. He was probably abused in some way, and in turn became abusive. My father displayed to his students that he was a caring, gentle, and a passionate mentor. No need to ask why he was such an abusive father and husband…he just was. This phenomenon is not as uncommon. Many people live dual lives; one that is transparent to outsiders and a deep, dark, secretive life to those they live with. I was abused, but the cycle ended with me.

    My father was cremated in May of 2009. I believe it was a few weeks later that I received a most peculiar phone call. It was from an unknown caller with a Chicago area code. When I answered the phone, there was an unfamiliar lady on the other line. The lady was visibly irritated.

Me: "Hello?"
Lady: "Hello Luther?"
Me: "Yes, who's calling?"
Lady: "Hello, I am Dexter's girlfriend. I wanted to talk to you about a few things. Do you have a minute?"
Me: "Yes, sure…what's up?"
Lady: "Do you know a lady named Kamilah?"
Me: "Yes, I dated her for a short time in college. Why do you ask?"
Lady: Well your brother is taking her out to a game. He told me to ignore the fact that he was flirting with her because he is trying to get dirt on you from her."
Me: "Damn! Does the craziness ever end? This is some Twilight Zone type of shit! First off, Kamilah really didn't know me. She can't tell Dexter anything about me that anyone else doesn't already know. Second of all, it all sounds like bullshit to me. Why would he go to her for knowledge about me?
Lady: "I knew it! He is so full of shit! He is always messing around on me! I am done with his ass! He calls himself a stripper but he uses his job to have sex with some of the people. One time I had to pick him up from a mansion where he had sex with a man! He gonna say that someone must have put something in his drink! Fuck him! I am done with his ass! He is all mad at me because the police took those text messages off my phone! He said I should have erased them. The cops surprised me at my house! I didn't have time to! My priority is my child!
Me: "I understand. Put your children first and everything will work out!"
Lady: "Thank you!"
Me: "Anytime…and good luck to you…bye."

FROM GOD'S MONSTER TO THE DEVIL'S ANGEL

She was a woman scorned. If she did have some dirt on Dexter, he had better be careful. A few weeks later Dexter's girlfriend called me again. It was nighttime. Her voice was visibly shaken.

Me: "Hey what's up?"

Lady: "Luther? Dexter and your cousin have been in my back yard looking into my house for over fifteen minutes! I think they are going to try something! Dexter thinks I have betrayed him!"

Me: "Betrayed him how? You didn't see the murder. You don't have any evidence against him…do you?"

Lady: "No…but I know they did it! He thinks I am working with the cops!"

Me: "If you fear for your life then call the cops."

Lady: "I called my cousins. They don't like Dexter anyway. They don't like the way he treats me. I did call the cops as well. I told them that Dexter put a box with what I think has bullets inside, under my bed. The box had drops of blood on it. The cops are sending a forensic team to get it in a few days."

Me: "It would take a few hours, but I could come up there if you really felt the need."

My wife was listening to our thirty minute conversation. I know that last statement irritated her. She's always telling me to stop fighting everybody's battles.

Lady: "No. It will be alright. I think Dexter and your cousin have left now. I will be moving in a few days. Dexter doesn't know where I am moving. Everyone is scared of Dexter. I feel comfortable talking to someone who he doesn't intimidate."

Me: "Ok. Good luck with your move and God Bless."

Whoever murdered Floyd "Bullet" Butler will never be mentally free. There were no witnesses and no recovered murder weapon. I never knew what happened with the forensic team and the box. I do know that when you do wrong, that thing called karma will be anxiously awaiting you. Dexter ended up getting arrested for armed robbery a few months after our father's memorial. Dexter told me that Telly and her husband removed a lot of valuables out of our father's house before moving back to Oklahoma.

About four months after my father's memorial, my mother died in the same house. I didn't care to inquire, but it was most definitely drug related or complications due to drug use. I didn't go to her funeral. I never knew her, and what I did know, I detested. My mother's drug addict boyfriend continued to live in the house after my mother passed. They left the bills for as long as they could in my father's name. Most of the bills were left outstanding. Everyone who took advantage of Floyd Butler's death will spend the rest of their miserable lives being opportunistic bottom feeders. That big beautiful house that my father owned was repossessed and later sold into foreclosure.

    It was revealed that my father wasn't getting payments from his land development firm. He took out almost $200,000 in home loans on his house. Before the home loans, the house was paid for. He died because he was misleading. People thought his firm was raking in money. The circling scavengers decided he was taking too long to die!

    I actually learned more about my father in death than when he was alive. My father never played a down for the Chicago Bears. He had a short stint, I believe as a practice team member. My father attended college at Northeastern State University in Oklahoma. Floyd "Bullet" Butler was inducted into their football hall. It was rumored that my father had another child who was younger than Ryan. I was never able to confirm it.

    My father started a foundation called Y.U.P.S. It stands for the Young Urban Preservationists Society. This non-for-profit organization taught inner city youths the importance of preserving the history of their community. It also enlightened on the goals of the historic society.

    What about me? Well, I am a hard working electrician. I am still married. My wife is my best friend, and our sons are my best men. We work hard and vacation as a family. Sometimes my wife and I get away to keep that spark. My sons are not abused, nor will they ever be. Our oldest two sons are in college and we have three boys to go. Wherever I go, my boys go with me.

    Monkey see, monkey do. The best gift I can give my sons is for them to see how a husband, father, and adult are supposed to behave. I never miss their games and I put their education first. I try to get involved with the community as much as I can. My doors are open to help tutor and mentor young men in my neighborhood. I volunteer at the local center called the Irving Center. A lot of young men need role models.

I am not my sons' friend, I am their parent. I instill in them integrity, honesty, discipline, hard work, love, and compassion. I can never make up for the wrong that I have committed in the past. But, since I left the streets, I will live with a purpose…to be part of the solution and not the problem.

If I can make it off the streets, anybody can. The first step is to stop accepting that you are a victim and take a proactive and positive role in your life. There are many people and organizations that will help, so don't be deterred by the ones who refuse to lend a helping hand.

I was thinking of a lot of different ways to end my book. Sayings like…'I may fail at my marriage, or I may fail at my job…but I will never fail as a father'. On the contrary, I will not fail at any of those things because of what it truly encompasses to be a good father. It is impossible to be a great father and have no desire to work. You can't claim to be a good dad and abuse the mother of your children.

Every day I carry the pain inflicted upon me, as well as the pain I have inflicted on others. This pain is a scar, just like the stab wound along my left side. It is a constant reminder of how I almost lost my life through negative conflicts. My scars, mental and physical, are a constant reminder of how far I have come.

It is said that the greatest teacher in life is your past mistakes…as long as you are willing to learn from them. From Justin to Mimi, it deeply saddens me that I allowed myself to go to such a dark place. I would give my life to undo the hurt that I have caused any of you. I will spend the rest of my life trying to stand as an example of how a male should carry himself, and atoning for my past transgressions.

"Never let your past imprison you, but rather allow it to empower you to inspire others"- Pacc Butler.

Visit my webpage for inspirational videos and blogs about the inner city at:

http://www.paccbutler.com/

Please rate my book on Amazon. This is invaluable to authors.

Coming soon···The Documentary *"Young Bulls"* ···for more information visit:

http://youngbulls.org/

www.ingramcontent.com/pod-product-compliance
Lightning Source LLC
Chambersburg PA
CBHW071926290426
44110CB00013B/1493